AEROBATICS

AEROBATICS

NEIL WILLIAMS

Illustrated by L. R. Williams

St. Martin's Press
New York

For information, write:
St. Martin's Press, Inc.
175 Fifth Avenue
New York
N.Y. 10010

Manufactured in the United States of America

Library of Congress Catalog Card Number: 78-19384
ISBN: 0-312-00756-6

First published in the United States of America in 1978

Foreword by

Air Commodore J. de M. Severne
MVO OBE AFC

Commandant, Central Flying School

Royal Air Force

There are several reasons for wanting to do aerobatics, but perhaps the most compelling are that they are challenging, exciting and above all enjoyable. Every pilot, whether he be amateur or professional, commercial or military, should have some degree of proficiency in aerobatics if, as the author says, he is to know the limits of his aeroplane and know how to get the best out of it.

I believe this is the first time that a comprehensive book on the art of aerobatics – and it is an art – has ever been written in any language and I am sure it will become a standard work for many years to come. Not only will it benefit the aspiring champion and all those who wish to improve their skill, at whatever level, but it will also benefit those who simply enjoy watching; just as a good hi-fi set and a degree of appreciation greatly enhance the enjoyment of listening to music, so will this book enable us all to appreciate the thought, effort and skill that goes into a competition sequence or a demonstration at an air display.

Few people are as well qualified to write this book as Neil Williams. He is a very experienced pilot in the broadest sense having flown over 150 types of aircraft, ranging from the 1912 Blackburn Monoplane to present-day military jets and modern airliners. He is also an experienced civil and military test pilot who knows better than anyone the importance of the cautious approach to flying. It is significant that, throughout his career, he has always retained the sheer joy of flying and anyone who has seen him perform in his Pitts Special will know that he is the ideal man to discuss aerobatics.

If you enjoy this book half as much as I did, you won't be able to put it down, so – read on!

Contents

Aerobatics

Introduction

This is a book, by a pilot, for pilots. It has been long in the planning, and longer still in the execution, because there have been questions which are also asked by the pilot about to try his hand for the first time at the sport of aerobatics – "how do I begin?" or "where shall I start?"

When·one knows a great deal about a subject, or when one knows very little, these problems arise.

Nearly twenty-five years ago, when I learned to fly, I asked these questions, but then there was no answer. A few pilots knew the absolute mastery of an aeroplane which is the reward of the aerobatic pilot, but very few would, or could, impart their knowledge. It was a closed shop.

Indeed, at that time aerobatics were the righteous preserve of the flying instructor, not something to be tampered with by an inexperienced club pilot. Well might those old pilots been proud of their prowess, long before the advent of Aresti, when exponents of the art such as Dusty Miller, of EFTS fame, could do things with a Tiger Moth that would make any modern pilot's hair stand on end. But now they are gone, and their skill with them. As a student pilot, I found myself in the same quandary as many students today; I desperately wanted to learn, but nobody would teach. I decided to teach myself.

So it was that sometimes, in those far off days, a Tiger Moth could occasionally be seen, at a great height over the coastal plain of South Wales, looping, stall-turning, spinning; cautiously at first, then with slowly increasing confidence.

Slow rolls took longer to learn; I had no instructor, no critic to watch me, nobody who even knew what I was doing: the official duty was usually "map reading exercises".

It was a foolish and painstaking way to learn, and many times it was only the strength and drag of the Tiger that saved me from more than embarrassment as I fell out of slow rolls, time and time again.

Finally I learned the secret of how to roll a Tiger accurately – but I had paid for it. This one manoeuvre had taken two and a half years to perfect! Gradually I added to my repertoire, and little by little came lower, but it was not until ten years after I had started that I finally came down as low as a thousand feet. In learning, I made nearly every mistake in the book, but I was lucky; and I tried to learn from them.

Now, nearly twenty-five years after those first struggling figures, I have learned something about this king of sports – the art of aerobatics. And now the boot is on the other foot, because in increasing numbers I am approached by pilots of different levels of experience, all asking the same question – will I teach them aerobatics?

Usually they want only a few flights, maybe up to five hours, and they cannot grasp the impossibility of trying to impart the knowledge of nearly a quarter of a century into so short a time. Even if I could instruct at that pace, they could not absorb it. A few dedicated pilots have accepted this, and are now beginning to see the results of their efforts reflected in their position in national and international competition, but these are the people who have made considerable sacrifices of time and money over a period of years.

For some pilots, aerobatic flying seems to be a short cut to the glamour and public acclaim of display flying, but this, for the competition pilot can be a dead end. He may well bask in the applause of the crowd, but a discerning observer will note the beginning of a deteriorating performance, unless at the same time one whets the edge of control with constant practice and actual competition. It is a hard existence; if it were easy everyone could do it. But in spite of this, there is actually no magic formula – it is simply a question of hard work. Perhaps the most difficult thing to acquire in the early stages is the knowledge of what is required, and the question of how and where to start. But no matter how much information is imparted by the written word, good instruction will always improve on theory. The aim of this book is to answer all the questions I wanted to ask when I started learning aerobatics, and to describe manoeuvres and sequences, basic and advanced. It is no substitute for good airborne instruction or even solo practice at a safe altitude. But it will tell you the best way of going about it, and the areas to avoid. In describing my own mistakes it will help you to progress more quickly, and more safely.

It all takes time, as does anything that is worth doing well. The tutor of Alexander the Great once remarked to his complaining pupil "There is no royal road to geometry." Neither is there a short cut to aerobatic flying.

1   *Why?*

For centuries, man watched with envy the flight of birds, and dreamed of being able to match their skill and grace. The unsteady, shaky flight of the earliest aircraft was a far cry from the effortless soaring of the birds, and far from being satisfied with their efforts, men still yearned for the same ease of control and manoeuvrability which persistently evaded their grasp.

Better aircraft with more reliable engines began to appear, and the pilots of these machines vied with one another at early flying demonstrations to prove the superiority of their craft. It was during such a meeting that the Frenchman Pegoud performed the first aerobatic manoeuvre when he looped his Bleriot. The First World War was responsible for a very rapid advance in the design of aircraft, and very soon it was found that the pilot with the more powerful and manoeuvrable aircraft would emerge victorious in air combat.

M. Adolphe Pegoud on his looping Bleriot Monoplane

At this time, pilots began to realise that the control, strength and power of the aeroplane could be made to conform to their will to produce an intricate pattern in the sky, giving them a sense of freedom that no man before them had ever enjoyed. They were flying with the ease of birds and the sport of aerobatics had been born.

Aerobatics soon became synonymous with stunt flying, unfortunately, and for many years was regarded as the wicked lady of aviation. Yet the lure of the pure aerial ballet remained and between the wars only a few timid pilots could resist the temptation to learn the art of aerobatics. At that time, the biplane reigned supreme, and unfortunate is the man who has not stopped to watch a tiny silver biplane high among the cumulus clouds, the sole performer on a stage of infinite breadth and indescribable grandeur. The roar of the engine is muted to a far-off drone, no louder than a bee in the summer sky, and the sun glints and sparkles on the wings and cowlings as the aircraft loops and rolls with easy grace.

How many thousands of unknown spectators are the audience to this performance? The pilot, oblivious to the envious watcher, sits behind a small windscreen, his hands and feet resting lightly on the controls. The air is crisp and clear and he is alone in the sky.

The sound is very different here, the muted drone is a deep-throated snarl that blends with the roar of the slipstream and the howl of the bracing wires. To the pilot this is no mere machine, but a living creature, quivering with life, eager to respond to every pressure on the controls. The slipstream thunders around the cockpit, tugging mischievously at the pilot's leather helmet and goggles. The propellor is a whirling disc, shimmering in the sun, and the instruments, trembling, tell their own stories – airspeed, altitude, engine rpm, oil pressure and temperature, fuel contents, sideslip. The pilot scans these at a glance, not really studying any one of them, but knowing that all is as it should be.

A slight back pressure on the stick and the aircraft soars upward, stick and rudder smoothly co-ordinated, and the little biplane is poised on a wingtip, the slipstream dying to a sigh while the engine noise becomes harsh and strident. Now the nose is dropping and the slipstream rises to a shrieking crescendo, drowning even the engine's blare. The controls become heavy as the airspeed indicator shows the speed rising towards the maximum. The pilot's movements are quite small now, for the aircraft responds very quickly to the slightest pressure.

Slowly the nose comes up and as the aircraft comes out of the dive, the pilot presses back harder on the stick. The machine arcs upward, the flying wires tight with strain, while the landing wires, relaxed, vibrate until they are blurred. The "*g*" forces press him down into his seat and his muscles are tensed as he combats the rising acceleration. Now the climb is vertical and the pilot looks up and back for the horizon to appear. The pull force is easier now and as the top wing comes into line with the horizon, the pilot eases the stick forward. With hardly a pause, the stick is pressed to the right and the horizon revolves slowly. A touch of right rudder and the roll off the top is complete. Another wingover, this time soaring above the peak of a snow white towering cumulus

Wing-Over

cloud, before diving again for a lazy, flowing, slow roll, so beauti-fully controlled and easy that the watchers on the ground are unaware of the months of practice to achieve it.

For most pilots, the sense of achievement and freedom is suf-ficient reward in itself – coupled with the knowledge that a pilot skilled in aerobatics is a much more accomplished pilot, since he knows the limits of his aeroplane and how to get the best out of it.

The art of aerobatics brings confidence and increases skill, touch, and an understanding of the finer points of aerodynamics – in a way that cannot be accomplished in any lecture room.

It is inevitable in such an advanced form of expression that those who excel will become interested in competition, for this is one way of determining just how good a pilot really is.

Competition flying is not a relaxing business, though, and many good aerobatic pilots prefer the enjoyment of flying for their own recreation rather than undergoing the pressures of contest flying.

For those who do enter competitions, there is all the colour and drama that anyone could wish for. At international meetings, pilots from fifteen to twenty countries arrive at the contest airfield with brilliantly painted machines.

Then comes the most enjoyable part; the training period, during which each competitor is allowed two practice flights over the airfield. Pilots walk up and down the lines of aircraft, renewing old acquaintances and making new ones. Occasionally one finds an aeroplane with a diagram of its pilot's aerobatic sequence attached to the panel and these are studied with interest. Some pilots with a strong sense of humour have been known to leave impossible sequences fixed to their aircraft and then to retire to a safe distance and watch the expression on their rivals' faces.

The waiting is the worst, especially for the first round of the competition. Many pilots at this stage ignore their rivals' performances and try to relax in their tents. Once in the aircraft, with the engine running, the initial nervousness disappears and one becomes impatient to get airborne. Preflight checks are usually carried out about three times each, because there must be no mistakes at this stage.

The starter's flag drops and we start the stopwatch. All nervousness has disappeared as we open the throttle for take-off. The climb is initially straight ahead, as the pre-aerobatic checks are carried out (one never sees a pilot showing off at a world championship event).

The climb pattern has been planned to put us at the correct height directly over the start point, marked by a cross on the ground. During the climb, we check to see if our four datum points are clearly visible on each end of each axis and we monitor our engine instruments.

We rock the wings – the signal that we are about to begin – and roll the aircraft into a dive straight above the main axis. Now we are almost over the centre of the field and can no longer see the axes. We think of those competitors who have a vision panel in the floor and resolve to modify our own aircraft. But there is no time now to think of that, we have full power selected. We make small and instinctive corrections for turbulence and after a quick check of the airspeed, the stick comes back hard and the aircraft shudders as the needle on the accelerometer peaks on the red line. The pitch is checked sharply as the aircraft hits the vertical and full right aileron is applied. The wingtips race around the horizon, which is blurred because of the high rate of roll. The datum points flash past — one, two, three, four — and the roll is checked exactly on the last one. The vertical climb is held until the speed is no longer reading and the power is cut right back to idle. As the aircraft starts to slide backwards, the stick is eased back a little and rudder and stick are then held as firmly as possible. The controls are trying to snatch over, and we hang on grimly. Suddenly the nose goes down hard in a vicious hammerhead stall; as it does, we apply full power, and as the engine roars back to life, we hit hard rudder and forward stick for a vertical diving outside flickroll. We cut the power again and recover after one turn, checking that our flight path is exactly vertical. We also note that we are exactly over the intersection of the axes; perhaps we don't need that clear vision panel after all!

So the sequence goes on for up to thirty manoeuvres of exacting precision flying, so different in concept from the antics of the little biplane high above the clouds, but equally as rewarding.

The combination of the two styles is probably the most exacting and difficult to achieve, and is the ultimate in aerial ballet. The effort is great, the concentration intense, the workload high, and the rewards infinite.

With each step, new vistas of knowledge and skill open up ahead; there is no place here for the man who professes to know it all. Here, with every freedom in space and time, man can satisfy his inner cravings, where science and art are blended into one, and where at last he can achieve mastery in the air.

2 *The raw material*

"If God had meant man to fly, he would have given us wings". So preached Bishop Wright, father of Orville and Wilbur, before his sons achieved the success that was to change the face of the world.

Yet, in a sense, Bishop Wright was correct, because the air is not man's natural element; he must always be an intruder. Pilots are made, not born. The "natural" pilot is really a myth, boosted by boy's adventure stories, and later, by the T.V. and film industry. What is really meant is that those individuals who have good physical and mental co-ordination will learn more quickly; and the RAF's accent on sport in the selection and training of pilots is indicative of this.

But there is no question of "supermen" here. Almost anyone can learn how to fly an aeroplane; indeed, at the time of writing, about 100,000 licences have been issued in this country. Why is it, then, that only a handful of pilots regularly fly advanced aerobatics.?

The primary fault lies in the bar or crewroom of the average flying club. It only requires a discussion to be started about stalling and spinning for the various "pundits" to go into nauseating detail about that horrific occasion when they were introduced to these exercises; and the detail will have lost nothing by repetition over the years. Student pilots will be alarmed by such stories, and a barrier will be raised in their minds which can effectively prohibit them from thinking and acting coherently when they eventually encounter that terror of the air, the spin.

I have trained pilots such as these, and others who have never been told that aerobatics are difficult, or dangerous, or make one feel unwell, and the second group learn much more quickly, and make better aerobatic pilots. I suppose it is impossible to suppress tales of fright and airsickness, because there seems to be some kind of morbid pleasure in the telling. It would appear to be "manly" to force oneself to overcome real fear, and to continue to try to keep up appearances, when in fact the last thing a student wants to do is to step into an aeroplane.

In the first place there is nothing wrong with being afraid of flying; lots of people who are extremely courageous in other spheres are not able to master their concern here. I am afraid of potholing — so I don't do it. In the same way, if there is a genuine fear of flying, the best thing to do is to find some other occupation. It is all very well proving how brave you are by continuing, but this can only be to the detriment of your instructor and other pilots. A frightened pilot will never fly as accurately or safely as he would want to. In any case, flying is supposed to be fun, so why pay a lot of money to be frightened?

In some cases, a student may have been frightened by being exposed to aerobatics poorly performed, at an unsafe altitude; and this can leave an indelible mark on his future piloting career. This is a different kind of fear, and this can be overcome by patient explanation, and a gentle introduction into well flown aerobatics at a safe height.

Mention aerobatics and the first reaction will be the possibility of airsickness. I am often asked after an aerobatic display if my stomach is still in good working order — and this question has even been asked by Air Force personnel; so how can one expect the average student or private pilot to react differently? It is certain that with regard to airsickness the biggest problem lies in the mind. One can experience nausea without actually moving one's body; the result of movement is the disorientation caused by the semi-circular canals in the ear. The physical result of these is the same and is directly traced to the brain, which also receives stimulus from the amount of pressure being exerted on the body, and the distribution of this pressure. For example, if one rides on a roller coaster at the seaside, when the car plunges down an incline, one's "stomach is left behind." But we know that the stomach does not move; so what causes the sensation? It is the result of change of pressure distribution from the seat to the floor, which transmits a message to the brain which says "I am falling". If one is now strapped securely to that same seat, and if one's feet are held clear of the floor, the sensation is no longer present. There is a jolt against the belt, and that is all. Now we have a parallel with a common problem in flying; either encountering turbulence or entering a dive suddenly. Merely tighten your seat belt and don't jam your feet hard on the floor, and the sinking sensation will disappear.

This same sensation is often present in a poorly demonstrated stalling exercise and is one of the reasons for the dislike of the exercise. It can of course be greatly reduced by the use of the above technique, but it can be eliminated altogether by a little thought on the part of the instructor.

For some reason, when the stall is approached, the nose is raised to an incredible angle, and before the stall proper is reached, the instructor heaves back on the stick and the aircraft rears up, everything goes quiet, and then gravity really takes over as the misused aircraft carries out the inevitable "hammerhead" stall. Down goes the nose with a bang, and another frightened and disillusioned student joins the ranks of the straight and level brigade.

There is absolutely no reason why this technique should be adopted; it doesn't teach the student what the accidental stall is really like, and if the aircraft won't stall properly then he should be shown on an aircraft that will, instead of having the wits scared out of him. I have had the task on many occasions of coaxing students into being shown a real stall after just such an experience. Invariably their reaction was "is that all it is?" And then they try it themselves; no more fears, no more "queasiness"; and more important, now they are more in command of the aeroplane.

Now, with the hurdle of stalling behind, the spinning exercise can be considered in a different light. Again with the stomach in mind, many students deliberately refrain from eating before spinning; the worst thing one can do. With an empty stomach grumbling away the student is not allowed to forget it, so that he is already psychologically prepared for disaster in that area. Also his blood sugar level will be lowered, and he will not have his normal workload and concentration capacity. During the recovery from the spin, the student will encounter positive acceleration in the order of $3g$ as the aircraft levels out. With an empty stomach this may cause him to "grey-out", especially if he is not used to g. Again this may cause him sufficient unpleasantness to deter him from wishing to repeat the experience, During hard training for aerobatics, if I find my g threshold reducing, I stop for a good meal, and allow an hour for the results to be effective. My g tolerance will then have gone up by at least 2. Perhaps the biggest fear in flying is that of falling; after all, the effects of gravity are dramatically imprinted on us all from a very early age. These fears are perhaps most noticeable in an open cockpit, where one feels much more in contact with the elements, and where one instinctively leans "against" the turn when the aeroplane banks. The best way to overcome this is in the knowledge that this is a perfectly natural reaction – this is, after all, not our natural element. If we consider that the forces involved can be likened to taking a corner on a motorcycle, it becomes apparent that we will not feel any strange effects if we lean with the machine. We will find, as we progress, that we can carry out simple aerobatic manoeuvres without feeling the need for restraining straps; indeed I have barrel-rolled aircraft without the crew knowing it!

Leaning with the machine

One needs to understand something of the construction of the aeroplane before one can feel any confidence in it; after all, it looks so frail compared, for example, to the family car. Just consider, though, what would happen to the family car if it were subjected to six times its normal weight!

Aerobatic aeroplanes, on the other hand, are regularly subjected to these forces, and do not exhibit any particular signs of stress. However, aerobatic aeroplanes tend to fly upside down, and if stalling and spinning caused problems, imagine the consternation produced by the thought of flying inverted, especially in an open cockpit aeroplane! What, one asks innocently, is the problem? Inevitably, it is the possible danger of falling out, and any assurances to the contrary will be met with the same scepticism that I would demonstrate, were I to be subjected to persuasion that potholing is safe! However, let us look at the facts. The difference between an open and closed cockpit, apart from the draught, is academic in that $\frac{1}{16}''$ perspex would be highly unlikely to retard one's progress. The only real difference is psychological. Current cockpit design provides for two separate harnesses, the primary one attached to the seat, and the secondary to the airframe itself.

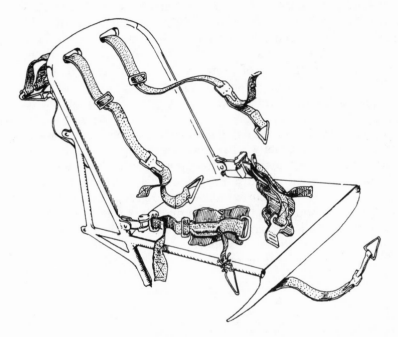

Typical aerobatic harness : ZLIN 526

The primary harness consists of five straps, including the all-important negative *g* strap, and these are secured by a simple clip, rather than a quick release box. At least one can see what is holding oneself in, and that it is properly done up. As insurance against the extremely unlikely event of the seat becoming detached, the secondary harness goes around both pilot and seat. This results in a total of seven restraining straps, each one capable of supporting about 3,000 lbs. Some years ago, as the result of a miscalculation, I had a rather abrupt encounter with terra firma, whilst attached to the aeroplane as described above. The result was a totally destroyed aeroplane, and a bruised, but intact, pilot. All seven straps had held, and although I parted company with the aeroplane after it hit the ground, I was still firmly strapped into the seat, and the secondary harness was still bolted onto what was left of the bottom longerons. A harness of this type will guarantee that one remains firmly attached to the aeroplane, no matter what.

These, then, are some of the initial problems encountered during the approach to aerobatics.

Before embarking on a course of aerobatic instruction, ask yourself why you want to do it. It will mean a considerable sacrifice, of time and money, at the least, and there will be no guarantee of results. If you see yourself as another Cantacuzene, better forget it, the law of averages exists, and he died in bed! If it's a question of impressing one's girl friend, by the time you are able to, the odds are she will have become fed up and moved on.

There is no reason for flying aerobatics; if you really want to, without knowing exactly why, and you are prepared to really work and to explore this exciting sport, you've been bitten. It is rather like a drug, the more you indulge, the greater is the attraction. But unlike a drug, there are no grey areas, only black or white. A famous Czechoslovakian pilot once said "You cannot lie to yourself in aerobatics" — here self discipline must reign supreme. Perhaps the most important thing that you will learn is the truth — pleasant or otherwise — about yourself.

3 *Preparation*

"How will I react"? is the question that is often asked by students about to embark upon their first aerobatic flight, for they cannot help comparing the thought of performing aerobatics with childhood memories of devilish fairground contrivances. Of all the hurdles they will have to cross, this is the first, and the hardest. A great many of their acquaintances will draw a depressing picture of the terrors in store; although a close investigation will reveal that they have little or no experience of aerobatic flying. This sport is the most misunderstood facet of aviation, so with this fact borne firmly in mind, the student should try to ignore the advice and comments of those not qualified to speak. It is a sad reflection on the state of the aeronautical community that pilots who should know better are guilty of prejudice in the field of aerobatics. Indeed, some may have had the uncomfortable experience of being subjected to aerobatics by someone whose enthusiasm exceeded their ability, and perhaps with a slack safety harness into the bargain!

If their introduction to the sport had been conducted in a more responsible manner, many more good pilots would have had the opportunity to increase their skills, and the sport would have been advanced by many years..

Initial doubts about one's reaction to unaccustomed stresses are easily resolved: on the first introduction to aerobatics the figures will be simple and the forces will not be excessive. To ensure that this is so one will have asked for a demonstration by a skilled and reliable pilot, who will at all times concern himself with the well being of his passenger. He knows that his potential student will be rather wound up, and he will limit both the duration and the content of the sortie to suit. In any case, fifteen minutes is quite long enough the first time up, since the aim is to provide an enjoyable experience. Let there be no worries about the physical forces of acceleration at this stage, since if one is fit enough to hold a pilots licence one can certainly accept the relatively modest accelerations involved, although when first encountered they will feel fairly high. The maximum negative *g* encountered will be one's own weight on the straps, since the instructor will not show anything more advanced than a slow roll on this flight. One will note that the straps restrain the body perfectly. In spite of the fact that the instructor adjusted the harness, the student will inevitably worry about his security, and this is quite a normal sensation at this stage. If one is concerned about this level of negative *g*, one can produce a worse situation on the ground by doing a handstand. In the aeroplane one assumes a sitting position, therefore there is less pressure on the chest and head. This is not in the least dangerous to any normal person.

With the demonstration flight behind us, it is now possible to look forward to being able to fly aerobatics oneself.

The first problem is to decide on the type of aeroplane to be used, a decision which will not arise if one elects to attend a local aerobatic course of instruction, as one will normally use the school machine. However, it is possible to make arrangements to bring along one's own machine to the school, or to hire machine and instructor separately. The most important aspect of this is to make sure that the instructor is really capable. A good instructor can teach well on a mediocre aeroplane; a mediocre instructor will never achieve results, even on the best aeroplane in the world. Bear in mind also, that just because someone is an instructor it doesn't mean that he is any good at aerobatics.

There is a wide variety of equipment to choose from, and the basic manoeuvres can be reasonably demonstrated in all of them, but here I have selected the Stampe SV4B as an example of a good basic and intermediate trainer, which can be, and is, currently used in all British competitions.

The use of such an aeroplane necessitates the purchase of various items of flying clothing; in any case if one is intending to fly aerobatics, these items will always be useful in other machines in the future.

Aerobatic aeroplanes tend to distribute oil with great impartiality, so in order to protect one's clothing a good flying suit is necessary. This should be light and comfortable, as even an open cockpit can get hot when the workload goes up. Zip or velchro pockets are essential for retaining loose cash, keys, etc. Never, never, fly aerobatics with loose articles in your pockets, which can find their way into control runs. If there is no alternative, tie them securely into a handkerchief.

The next item is a good helmet, close fitting, and with ventilation holes if possible. This may be augmented by a bone-dome, which although a little cumbersome could make all the difference in an accident.

I know of a pilot who received slight injuries when another aircraft taxied into his machine. His bone-dome saved his life. Make sure that the retaining straps of headgear are securely fitted, and ensure that the bone-dome is the correct size.

An oxygen mask with microphone is generally better for communication as a throat mike doesn't operate well in an open cockpit. A good pair of gloves is essential, not only for protection, but also to ensure that one's hand does not slip from the control column, and finally a good set of goggles should be bought. These should afford a good field of vision, and should be tight enough to resist the effects of slipstream. I personally use Mk 8 RAF goggles, with parachute elastic. Even in a closed cockpit, goggles should be carried, as a precaution.

The most expensive item of equipment for the aerobatic pilot is a parachute; and here one must decide on one's priorities. If one is flying, as one should, above 3,000 feet, during the course of instruction, it is sensible to carry a parachute, in the same way that one takes out insurance before travelling on an airline; not with any intent, but just in case.

With the pilot now suitably equipped, let us look at the aeroplane. A good pre-flight inspection is essential before each flight, as the aerobatic aeroplane is worked hard. One gets to know the areas which require specific attention on each type. At the end of a day's flying the aeroplane should be thoroughly cleaned, not only because if oil is left on the surfaces, they will deteriorate, but also because it is the one way of ensuring that every square inch of the aeroplane is examined. The accelerometer is not reset by the last pilot, but is left for the next pilot to see, so that he knows how hard the machine has been flown. Oil and fuel are especially important, as an aerobatic aircraft can get through these commodities remarkably quickly. On some types, dual instruction cannot be given if the fuel tank is full, while on others the inverted system will not run unless the tank is full.

The safety harness should be examined carefully for fraying and oil contamination. The Stampe in particular tends to have its cockpit floor liberally coated with oil, and this should be wiped up. A soft cushion should never be used for aerobatics, as it will compress under *g* and cause the harness to slacken off. It will also put a strain on the spine during high *g* manoeuvres, and will create a feeling of insecurity generally. A rock hard cushion is not so comfortable in the cruise, but it will improve your feel for the machine in aerobatics: a parachute gets rid of the problem, as it is designed to fit into the seat pan.

There are different combinations of connecting the straps, but experience has indicated that the best method is to start with the seat fully down. The secondary harness (connected to the airframe) and the adjustable negative *g* strap are then connected, and the combination is pulled as tight as possible. This is where most people run into trouble; they tend not to tighten the harness sufficiently: it should be so tight that it almost hurts. It will ease off in flight to a comfortable and secure level. Next the primary harness is tightened in the same way, so that one is left absolutely immobile and not a little breathless. Finally, the seat is raised one or two notches, which has the effect of tightening the lower straps even more. I cannot place too much emphasis on the need to be securely and tightly strapped in. Even so, all the straps will loosen off in flight but will still result in the pilot being very firmly restrained in the pelvic area, which is close to the pilots own centre of gravity. The pressure of the straps across the chest will have eased off, and this is very important for inverted flight, where nearly all the weight is on the negative *g* strap, and the shoulder straps serve merely to stabilise the upper body. If these shoulder straps were too tight they would tend to restrict breathing during inverted flight and would cause the pilot to tend to hold his breath. This would result in an increase of blood pressure to the head, and could result in an increase in the value of negative *g* being experienced, so that although the accelerometer might show $-2g$ during an inverted turn, the pilots upper body and head might well be subjected to $-4g$, with the attendant distress. The real secret of combating negative *g*, as we will find out later, is to relax.

With the pilot firmly strapped in he must ensure that he is as comfortable as possible, as any distraction will reduce his learning potential; and he must be able to reach all controls and to move them easily throughout their range. This sounds very basic, but it is surprising how many pilots either can't see (sitting too low) or perch themselves so high that they couldn't possibly reach full rudder.

At last, firmly installed, the pilots reaction is that he is an integral part of the aeroplane; but now he must consider this in a different sense, that is, that the aeroplane is now an extension of himself. It is now not going to be a question of moving the controls and the aeroplane does his bidding; he and his aircraft must operate as one integral combination.'

4   Pre-aerobatic training

Strangely enough, the initial exercise can be carried out on any type of aeroplane, even commercial types, for this is revision of the first thing all of us learned in the air; straight and level flight. "What has this got to do with aerobatics"? One might ask; and the answer is that it forms the basis of all competitive manoeuvres. Given a fairly constant weight it follows that for straight and level flight at varying airspeeds, there will be a noticeable change in aircraft attitude, and since the speed will vary from stalling speed up to VNE, the aircraft will therefore be

Maximum and minimum attitudes for straight and level flight

subject to the maximum attitude change. For example, flying off level from the top of a vertical roll is going to produce a very different attitude from the high speed horizontal line which preceded the manoeuvre. It will be seen, therefore, that one must obtain the instinctive knowledge that the selected attitude at any given speed will result in level flight. The demonstration of two speeds for a given power setting, reducing to the attainment of the minimum drag speed, forgotten by most private pilots, now assumes new significance. Obviously, when the minimum drag speed has been found, it follows that if the aircraft can be held for reasonably long periods near this speed, at full power, during a sequence, the engine will be able to impart the maximum energy to the aircraft, in terms of kinetic or potential energy, and the importance of this will be seen later.

Co-ordination and confidence are all important in aerobatics, and an excellent exercise for these is to fly alternate 360° turns, using at least 60° bank, with maximum aileron being used in the rolls in and out, and in the turn reversals. The aim here is to keep the slip ball firmly centred throughout, and not to gain or lose any height at all. For every second spent in scanning the instruments, nine seconds should be spent with the head "out of the cockpit". In aerobatics, one is traversing a large area of sky, with rapid direction alterations, and a good lookout is essential. These turns are a good loosening-up exercise prior to aerobatics, and can be very satisfying to perform when the jolt of one's own slipstream confirms a perfect manoeuvre.

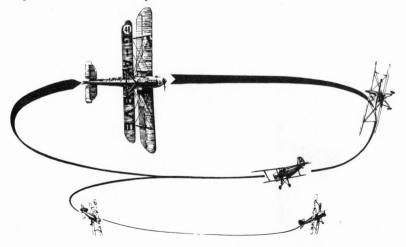

360s – clearing turns

Before going on to basic aerobatics it is as well to revise stalling and spinning, as both of these manoeuvres will be utilised extensively in the future. They are not merely an exercise to be accomplished with a feeling of relief, they are the tools of the trade and must be tamed and made to conform to one's wishes. Allied to these is the control of the aeroplane at the absolute minimum speed, since for a large part of the time in aerobatics the speed will be near or below the stall, and a quick and sensitive touch is required.

A good look-out is essential

In slow flight, a constant height is maintained, and the speed reduced until the aeroplane is barely flying. Each time a wing tries to drop it must be corrected with rudder, and with a little extra power to offset the drag. Here an important lesson will be learned; if aileron is used, the wing will continue to drop, as the down-going aileron causes the wingtip to stall. Once the aeroplane partially stalls, it will be seen that one has to reduce the angle of attack noticeably before the airflow once again becomes laminar. This would of course lose marks in a competition, where an alternative method would be to jerk the stick forwards and back again quite quickly. Not taught in any flying school, this can often cause the errant airflow to reattach itself, whereupon the existing airspeed will be sufficient to allow level, controlled flight. It is important that this be done at a safe height, as it is not 100 per cent effective; though it is worth trying, in a competition, to save a manoeuvre, such as flying off level from a vertical roll.

Slow flying again breeds confidence through the knowledge of exactly what the aircraft will and will not do. With plenty of height it does not matter if the aircraft stalls, and recovery from this can be practiced until it becomes fully automatic. I once had the pressure instruments fail in a jet aircraft, and I was led back for a formation landing. On short finals, with no ASI, the other aircraft overshot and gave me the full benefit of his slipstream, whereupon my aircraft flicked through 90°. It would have gone further but for the fact that I had instinctively applied full opposite rudder and forward stick; it was one of the many occasions when I have been saved by the ability to fly aerobatics.

Although it is quite likely that the spin will be encountered accidentally in aerobatics, it can also be used deliberately as a precision manoeuvre. Spinning is perhaps the most maligned aspect of light aeroplane flying, and for many pilots it assumes the malevolent proportions of the first World War, when it was first called Parke's Dive after the aviator who first survived it, and recorded his recovery actions. There is quite a lot involved in the technicalities of a spin, so suffice it to say that the character of the spin is generally an integral part of the aeroplane's behaviour. It is made up partly of the ratio of the pitching inertia against the rolling inertia, the shape of the keel area and its distribution, the position of the controls, the gyroscopic force of the engine and propellor, and the CG. Since we cannot do very much about the basic shape of the aeroplane, only the last three need concern us. Two of these are under control of the pilot in the air, the third must be attended to before take-off, i.e. the position of the centre of gravity.

Wake turbulence

If the CG is beyond the aft limit there exists a possibility that the spin may go flat, with the attendant problem of prolonged recovery. With the Stampe, the main thing to ensure is that there is nothing in the luggage compartment. If you are not sure about your aircraft's limits, look it up in the Flight Manual. Some aircraft may be restricted in the number of turns they are allowed to do.

'Parkes Dive' at Larkhill

Many aerobatic aircraft have the CG as far back as possible, within the limits, so that they have lower pitch stability. This gives them better pitch response, more control authority, and lighter control forces. It also gives a flatter spin.

To start with, it is better to have the CG rather more forward, although with the Stampe, for example, having emptied the lockers, there is not much more adjustment easily available. It is likely that when the spin was demonstrated during the syllabus for the PPL it resulted in the aircraft being pulled up into a steep climbing attitude, and then full rudder being applied. The effect would be a half flick roll to the inverted position, after which the nose would drop, with hardly any rotation. Then, the rotation would come back with a vengeance, and the aircraft would accelerate into an oscillatory spin. No wonder so many students are put off.

The precision aerobatic spin is a very different manoeuvre. Here the aircraft maintains level flight as it decelerates, with the angle of attack gently increasing as the airspeed drops. With the knowledge that the stalling speed is 38 knots, as it reaches 40, left rudder is applied smoothly and steadily, and the aircraft starts to roll to the left as the stall is reached. As the wing and nose start down, the stick is pulled firmly and steadily back. The result is a very smooth transition into a spin which is stable within half a turn of entry; there is no confusion or disorientation; the whole process is extremely gentle. Recovery is initiated with half a turn left to go to the desired exit heading, and

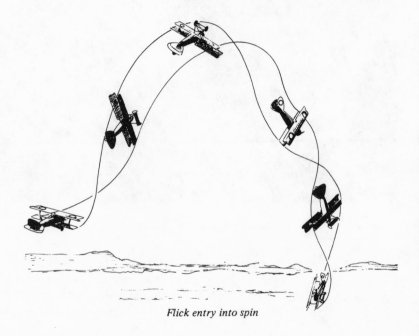

Flick entry into spin

Competition spin entry

consists of full rudder to oppose the yaw (in this case right rudder), pause, then stick smartly forward, as far as is necessary to stop the rotation. On some aircraft, full forward stick may be necessary. The spin should then stop at the correct point, whereupon all controls are centralised. As a result of the stick having been moved smartly, the exit dive angle should be vertical, and this is where we see a difference from the PPL spin, because, in competition, marks are gained not only from the smooth entry, exact rotation, and clean stop, but also from the vertical exit line. Another difference lies in the fact that the throttle is opened wide as soon as the rotation has stopped, to allow the aeroplane to make a clean, hard exit into horizontal flight, with high airspeed, ready for the next manoeuvre.

If the inverted fuel system is selected, it will prohibit the throttle from being fully closed, otherwise the engine may stop. There are two conflicting requirements in this case; to reduce rpm as much as possible to prevent undue gyroscopic force, and yet using enough throttle to keep the engine going. Fortunately, the worst that will happen with the Stampe is that manipulation of the throttle in the spin may cause a change in rotation which will make the aircraft overshoot the intended heading. With a direction of propellor rotation anti-clockwise as seen from the cockpit, any increase of rpm will tend to flatten the spin if the spin is to the right, and vice versa. This is due to the gyroscopic yaw effects being felt 90° in the direction of propellor rotation, and causing a pitch up. So it will be seen that increased rpm will pull the nose down in a left hand spin. Of course the opposite applies with an engine which turns clockwise as seen from the cockpit.

On some aircraft, such as the Zlin, which has a large, heavy propellor, and some considerable distance from its disc to the CG, it may not recover from a right hand spin unless the throttle is fully closed.

During all normal spinning the ailerons are held central, as on some types they will tend to trail in the direction of roll. It is especially important that the ailerons are not involuntarily used during the spin exit; should this use be required in the event of an emergency then they must be used positively. On most aerobatic aeroplanes they will not be needed, but in a contrary situation aileron should be applied in the direction of roll, whilst all the time maintaining rudder opposite to the yaw and full forward stick. The rate of turn indicator will always show the true direction of yaw, regardless of whether the spin is erect or inverted. The slip ball should be ignored completely. In the normal erect spin, the use of ailerons will change the character of the spin. When outspin aileron, i.e. aileron opposite to the direction of the spin, is applied with the Stampe, the nose rises from 40° to about 30° below the horizon, and the wings are level. With inspin aileron the nose goes down to 45° and the spin is faster and tighter.

It is interesting to experiment, given plenty of height, because the docile behaviour of this aircraft nevertheless gives a pointer to the sort of characteristics produced by the effects of aileron.

It is important not to move the head about unnecessarily during the spin, because one can suffer coriolis effects which can produce severe disorientation.

It is best to look straight over the nose of the aeroplane in the erect spin, and in a multi-turn spin I find that it helps in orientation to call the number of turns aloud to myself.

In spinning, as a precision manoeuvre, there is a risk of a phenomenon which resembles self-hypnosis, and this must be guarded against. What usually happens is this. The pilot requires to carry out a multi-turn spin, but during the early stages of the spin, his attention is distracted, perhaps by attempts to set up the idling RPM. The result is that he misses his exit point, and realises that if he pulls out in the wrong direction he will get zero for the manoeuvre; so he elects to do another turn, and to recover next time round. If he misses it this time, he is now really getting confused and says to himself "I'll get it next time" — "No, missed, next time" and so on. The further this performance is allowed to continue, the worse it gets, and one does not appreciate how low one is getting, until the ground starts to open out, and then it may be too late. This situation can be aggravated by having less than a whole number of turns, e.g. one and three quarters, as one tends to lose one's primary exit line. If this occurs one must make a concentrated effort to carry out the correct recovery immediately, regardless of what heading the aeroplane comes out on. In the case of extreme disorientation, the Stampe will usually recover if all the controls are centralised, but if this technique is adopted it is best to look down into the cockpit to make sure that everything really is central.

Merely releasing the controls will not ensure recovery as the rudder tends to trail in-spin. With the Stampe, indeed with most light aeroplanes, the position of the rudder is critical. Some people make the mistake of trimming into the stall prior to the spin, and this can result in quite a heavy push force being required in recovery. Occasionally when one thinks the stick is fully forward, an extra push will produce an additional movement which may make all the difference.

If, during recovery, the stick is moved forward slowly, the spin will apparently speed up considerably before stopping. The reason for this is that in the stable spin there is a balance between the couples of roll and yaw. When the yaw is reduced by applying opposite rudder, the energy content of the aeroplane causes the roll rate to increase, until the couple is finally broken, and the spin stops. Another factor is that the upgoing wing unstalls completely and adds to the autorotation.

In any spin of short duration the character of the spin will be primarily determined by the method of entry, so since competition spins are usually not more than two turns, the value of a smooth entry cannot be over-emphasized.

The more exotic forms of spinning will be covered later. It remains only to experience inverted flying, and the method of recovery from the vertical and we are ready to commence the basic manoeuvres.

During the demonstration of inverted flying, the student will appreciate why the straps were pulled so tightly on the ground. Now, they are quite comfortable, and he is held quite firmly down onto the cushion or parachute. He will also appreciate that "up" and "down" are referred to in relation to himself and not to the now inverted Earth. If he did not remember to tuck away all loose strap ends, he will now be embarrassed by seeing them dangling in front of his eyes.

This is a stable aeroplane, and the instructor will draw his attention to the fact that it is now trimmed fully nose heavy. Nothing can be done about the dihedral, so the aeroplane will now be laterally unstable while it is inverted. The student will also appreciate the fact that the engine continues to run steadily on the inverted fuel system.

Usually the student is reluctant to move any of the controls because he will think that their function is reversed, due to being inverted. I usually tell the student to hold the controls lightly and to use them in the natural sense, because of course they operate in the same sense that they always did. He will probably make the mistake of clutching the control column as though his life depended on it, and I find that the best approach is to take control and to get him to hold both arms "above" his head. Now, with all his weight on the straps, he suddenly realises that he is not going to fall out, and when he returns to the controls his touch is much lighter. This method always works, although I don't understand the psychology behind it, and it provides the confidence necessary to progress to the next stage.

The recovery from the vertical is merely to cater for a stall turn attempt which has gone wrong. If one appreciates sufficiently early that a stall turn isn't going to work, it is best to apply full rudder, pull the stick back, and allow the aircraft to fall into a spin, from which one can then recover. If one delays too long, the result can be an inadvertent tailslide, with the possibility of damage. I once got it wrong in a Tiger Moth, and slid backwards nearly 400 feet with full rudder jammed on — I couldn't get it off. The aircraft had tilted in the direction of the rudder, and the two forces were exactly balanced. There was a loud bang before the nose dropped, and I landed to find that I had broken every rib in the rudder. So the tailslide is not to be taken lightly. If one is going to slide, leave full power on to cushion it, and hang on tight to stick and rudder, and try to stop any deflection of these controls. Once you know what to expect, it is not too difficult to keep things in the middle until the nose drops, which it will do, in the same way that if a throwing dart is dropped point up, it will tip nose down before it has fallen very far. The deliberate tailslide is learned a good deal later.

At this point one has passed through the initiation stage, and the way ahead is now clear. A thorough briefing before and after each flight, and a good grounding in the theory of flight will add interest and stimulate enthusiasm. Now we are ready to fly aerobatics!

5   The basic manoeuvres - the loop

Look in the latest version of the Aresti aerobatic dictionary and you will find approximately 100,000 different aerobatic manoeuvres! It is not until one examines this book in detail that one appreciates the endless possibilities of combination manoeuvres which refute one's initial comment of "impossible". Not only possible, but established fact, and all of them stemming from only four basic figures!

All aerobatics have as their foundation stones the loop, roll, stall turn, and spin. Next time you see an aerobatic sequence, try and bear that statement in mind; you will find that it is absolutely true.

It therefore follows that if one can master these four properly, there is no limit to what one can achieve, within the performance capability of one's aeroplane. The manoeuvres described in this book are not the ones taught at the average flying clubs, or even in the RAF. From the beginning we will concentrate on competition style figures on which we can build in the future.

The spin has already been discussed, so the remaining three manoeuvres can now be looked at, and of these, the stall turn requires a fine sense of timing, so it is best left until the end, by which time we will have acquired some skill and confidence in the loop and roll.

In my younger days I always thought that the loop looked fairly easy, so I determined that as soon as I was allowed away from the field solo, I would attempt one. So it was that on one fine summer's evening I climbed to a great height, gathered my courage, dived to an incredible speed, and hauled back on the stick. The ensuing manoeuvre puzzled me not a little, after I got it sorted out. In retrospect it would seem that I flicked out at the top. I was doubly chastened when I got back to the field because although the sun was still shining at 5,000 feet, down below it was getting dark. When I finally managed to get it on the ground, I was treated to a short interview by my instructor who, fortunately didn't know about my attempted loop. Not a very auspicious beginning for a budding aerobatic career.

The basic loop is, in fact, very easy; so much so that I often wonder how I managed to make such a mess of it on that summer's evening; and I couldn't really ask my instructor, after that episode! Since then, I have found a technique of teaching which allows a student to learn the manoeuvre in a very short time.

First one sets up the aircraft in a fast cruise condition. Then, the machine is trimmed slightly nose heavy, so that it can be held in level flight with only the pressure of one finger. Next, the throttle is opened wide, and the aircraft is dived until the rpm reaches the maximum permissible, and a note is made of the airspeed, which on the Stampe will be about 120 knots. Speed is now reduced, and the aircraft is climbed back to the required height, but without retrimming. The trim is now set for all aerobatic flying, and although many pilots use the trimmer during manoeuvres to take the load off the stick, I prefer to accept these loads, because it gives me a feedback of information from the aeroplane, and a datum to work from. If the stick force changes unaccountably it may mean that something on the aircraft has moved, and I must then land and investigate.

Also I know that with a fixed pitch propellor as long as I do not exceed 120 knots I cannot possibly over-rev the engine, so that is one less instrument I have to monitor. If I reach and exceed 120 knots I know I have to start throttling back, and after that I must once again refer to the rpm gauge until the speed falls again. During the climb up there is ample time to look around for other aircraft in the vicinity.

Now we need to know the speeds required for the various manoeuvres. We know that the stalling speed is 38 knots so we will round it off to 40 knots. Two and a half times this speed will give us the correct speed for loops, barrel rolls, hesitation rolls, slow rolls, stall turns, Cuban eights and reverse Cuban eights. Three times the speed will permit a roll-off-the-top or a half vertical roll.

Exactly twice the real stalling speed will give the absolute maximum flick roll speed, i.e. 76 knots, but to cater for ASI error and pilot mistiming, it is better to use 70 knots. This formula is correct for most light aeroplanes.

The speed in this case for a loop is 100 knots. It will help to select a line feature on the ground so that one can assess accuracy and maintain orientation, and this line feature, e.g. railway, road, canal, etc., should be also aligned with the prevailing wind.

Make sure that you are not over a built up area, and that there is a good reference feature nearby, e.g. a lake; as it is only too easy to drift downwind and get lost when performing aerobatics. Of course you will have a map of the area in the pocket of your flying suit!

The object is to fly the aircraft around a circular flightpath whose plane is vertical. The pilot's head will be pointing towards the centre of the circle, and the start and finish of the manoeuvre will be at the bottom of the loop.

The primary control used in this figure is the elevator, with the rudder and ailerons being used to maintain the plane of the manoeuvre.

Align the aircraft into wind above the line feature, and open the throttle wide. Keeping the wings level and the slip ball in the middle, allow the aeroplane to accelerate to 100 knots, then re-establish level flight momentarily.

This is in preparation for competition work later, when the establishment of level flight between the manoeuvres indicates to the judges where one figure ends and the next begins.

A final check that the slip ball is central and the stick is pressed firmly backwards. As the *g* builds up, press the abdominal muscles hard against the lap straps; although the *g* will not exceed 4, this is enough to cause greyout if one is relaxed and not used to it.

In addition we must guard against the slightest "tunnel vision" effects, because at this stage we are looking firmly to the front, relying on peripheral vision for any unwanted roll information. As the aircraft reaches about 70° of pitch, the pressure on the stick is eased slightly, and we now transfer our attention to the wingtips as the *g* lessens. The reason for the initial *g* being as high as 4 is because we are flying a perfectly round loop. We look at each wingtip in turn, several times, because, if we look at only one, we will automatically roll in that direction. We keep the wingtips in the same relationship to each other with respect to the horizon, and simultaneously ease off the back pressure more and more as we approach the inverted position; and here the nose heavy trim helps us. We correct any errors at this stage with tiny co-ordinated movements of ailerons and rudder. Now we can throw the head back until we can see the horizon, and can identify the now inverted line feature. With less than our own weight on the seat we float gently across the top of the loop, using ailerons and rudder in a co-ordinated manner to track the nose exactly along the line feature. Still with full power left on, although the airspeed is starting to rise, we do not hurry, because we must let the aircraft fly out to round off the loop. We noticed as we came over the top, that the speed was below stalling speed, but since we are under less than one *g*, the aircraft did not stall.

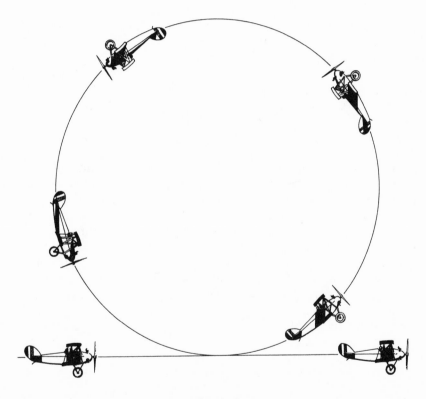

Ref. P.30 The Loop

We will find in aerobatics that the indicated speed becomes less and less important; only the angle of attack is of interest to us. Now, as we approach the vertical dive, we start increasing the pressure on the stick again, harder and harder but being careful not to stall; bracing against the rising *g*, still harder, and the aircraft is no longer accelerating, even with full power, because

The Loop entry 'Correct and Incorrect'

we have now balanced thrust and gravity with profile and induced drag. As we reach the bottom of the loop the aeroplane is held cleanly in level flight to mark the completion of the figure, and in the same instant we hit our slipstream, so we know that the start and finish were in the same place. Had we encountered the slipstream whilst still in the dive it would have told us that we had flown a tall, egg-shaped loop, and this would have also been marked by a fairly constant pitch rate around the loop. Because of our changing airspeed we must have a high pitch rate at the bottom, when the speed is high, and conversely, a very low pitch rate across the top. Although we will consider gyroscopic and slipstream effects later, it is better at this stage to aim for an entirely visual adjustment, whilst at the same time trying to relate the tiny slipping and yawing effects which can just be detected to the visual corrections we have to make.

Now it is all very well to describe a near perfect loop, but it is unlikely that one's first attempt will be crowned with success, as I know only too well from my own experience!

The two major faults are to be found in the initial pitch rate: one tends to pull either too hard, or not hard enough. In the first case, the *g* on entry will be too high, with the associated "tunnel vision", then as the aircraft passes the vertical, if it has good aerodynamic stall warning, it will start to buffet.

Both the high g and buffet will cause drag, and during the buffet itself the elevator will lose some of its power, thus reducing the pitch rate. If the aircraft does not have good stall warning, the first you will know of the error is that the machine will flickroll smartly out of the top of the loop.

To give two examples, the Chipmunk will buffet if it is pulled to tight; while the Harvard will flick.

The second common error in the loop is not to pull tight enough, which results in the aircraft running out of speed and falling out of the top of the loop. It should be noted that although the aircraft might stall when it is inverted, as long as the stick is aft of neutral there will be no possibility of an inverted spin, and this is something which concerns students. Reference to the chapter on advanced spinning will explain this statement.

If the aircraft stalls, flicks, or simply falls out of the top of a loop, don't panic, there is no need to do anything quickly. Remember that we are flying above 3,000 feet, and that airspace is there for a reason; it is our insurance policy. Wait until the aeroplane develops a recognised flight condition, e.g. spin, spiral, and then recover. In competition aerobatics the power is left on more than in the style taught in the RAF. This is because eventually the aeroplane will be operating at low level and every time the throttle is closed we sacrifice performance. Also, by maintaining full power, we have more lift and control due to the propellor blast, and finally, we do not have the sudden directional changes due to slipstream and gyroscopic effects. Rather than throttle back on the way down, we keep the speed under control by pulling more g, and the resulting increase in induced drag gives good speed control. We can demonstrate that from cruising inverted flight we can pull down into the second half of a loop, using full power, and only achieve a 10 knot increase in airspeed.

At this early stage it is quite common to have an error in roll on the way up into a loop; this may be caused by turning the head too early, or only looking in one direction. One automatically tends to incline the stick in the direction in which one is looking. Also, if one is sitting on top of the controls, or too far away, one's own personal geometry results in an aileron input during a pitching manoeuvre. This is why so much attention must be paid to seating position on the ground.

If such an error appears, it will just be noticed when the aircraft, reaches the inverted position, and the student sees that the wings are not parallel to the horizon. With no time to think about it, he will either do nothing or even make the wrong correction. In normal erect flight he would have no problem, and the situation is really the same here; one merely aligns the wings with aileron, and keeps straight with the rudder. An alternative method is to make the correction gradually in the second half of the loop. But the real solution is to find out why the aircraft has lost direction in the first place, and to correct this situation. Another source of error is misuse of rudder, and this will be covered in the chapter on gyroscopics. At this stage, it is best to ensure that with the wings level, at the start of the loop, the slip ball is in the centre. The rudder can then effectively be frozen for the first part of the loop; we will go deeper into the finesse of rudder later.

Ideally one should have the same speed and height at the exit as were present during entry: this will allow the next manoeuvre to be entered immediately, without having to dive for more speed. At this stage, it is a good idea to get used to monitoring the engine instruments, as one doesn't want to operate the engine without oil pressure, for example. At the same time we should acclimatise ourselves to the sound of the engine; if the note changes at all, it could herald trouble. When you get to know it, the engine will practically "talk" to you. I well remember an occasion when a pilot wore a helmet with more sound-proofing than he was used to. The variable pitch propellor chose that flight to overspeed, and with the new helmet deadening the noise, the result was a badly over-revved engine which took two months to repair.

An aeroplane will nearly always give you a hint of trouble, if you are alert and listening for it.

The first time out, don't do more than six to ten loops, because by then you will be getting a little tired, and you may start to make mistakes; and it is important at this stage to be sufficiently alert to appreciate what has gone wrong, and to correct it. If you start off well, it will give you confidence: if not, remember that everybody has a bad day; and it may be better to land and try again tomorrow.

6 *The basic manoeuvres – the roll*

The slow roll is one of the most satisfying manoeuvres to perform well; equally it requires more co-ordination than any of the other basic manoeuvres, and for this reason it usually gives the student more trouble in the early stages of leaving. As with all aerobatics, there is no substitute for good instruction in the air, as I found to my cost when I taught myself slow rolls from a book, and took two and a half years in the process. Since then, two things have struck me over the years; first, when trying to explain the manoeuvre in black and white, most instructors plunge straight in at the deep end, and talk about "top rudder, bottom rudder, etc." until the student is so confused that he can barely fly straight and level. There are so many parameters to be considered in such a short time that it is small wonder that most pilots never really master the slow roll.

In the second place, if you talk to a dozen instructors, you will be told a dozen different methods of flying a slow roll! The important thing to realise is that all of them may be correct — for that particular instructor. The method that works for one person will not necessarily fit in with another's style, and here the student must be encouraged to find his own style. The only criteria must be that it looks correct from the ground.

The method I now adopt to teach the slow roll has been proven many times to produce the best results in the shortest time; and this will therefore give a psychological boost to the student. Confidence is, after all, one of the most important aspects of learning in aerobatics, and knowledge breeds confidence. By this method a student will be able to fly a very passable slow roll after only 30 minutes instruction, but bear in mind that the real finesse will still have to be learned.

Aresti defines the slow roll as a 360° rotation about the longitudinal axis of less than 15 seconds duration. More than 15 seconds would qualify for a "superslow roll". He goes on to state that these rolls can be carried out at every angle, e.g. 45°, vertical, and so on.

We will confine ourselves to the conventional slow roll in horizontal flight, the aim being to roll the aeroplane around its longitudinal axis by means of the ailerons, and using the elevators and rudder to maintain height and direction. During the roll, it follows that the aircraft will be in true inverted flight half way through the roll, so that all the pilot's weight will be on the straps, which must therefore be properly tightened so that there is no relative movement between pilot and aeroplane. It will be an advantage if the engine continues to run in inverted flight, as it will on the Stampe, although the slow roll can be learned with a non-inverted fuel system aeroplane.

All the normal precautions are taken, including the pre-aerobatic checks. It doesn't matter which checklist is used, as long as all the points are covered. My own checklist is as follows:

Rudder, seat, harness	— adjusted
Controls	— Full and free
Fuel	— ON, inverted and sufficient
Airframe	— Clean, gyros caged.
Cockpit	— No loose articles.
Lookout, altitude, locality	— Satisfactory.

The aircraft is then trimmed for aerobatics as previously described, and with an entry speed of 100 knots, there is no need to dive, if we use full power. Although we are using two and a half times stalling speed, we will later discover that the Stampe can be rolled at only one and a half times stall speed, so there is evidently plenty of speed in hand.

It will help initially if we can select a distant point, perhaps a cloud near the horizon, on which we can keep straight.

To begin with, we will fly a simple aileron roll, to build up confidence. We remember that before we commenced a loop, we established level flight, with the slip ball central, and wings level, and we do exactly the same here, at 100 knots. Clamp the feet firmly to the rudder pedals, and do not move them! The rudder causes more problems in the slow roll than anything else, so to begin with we will dispense with it.

Lift the nose to about 20° above the horizon, and then check the pitch, before doing anything else. Many students seem to have trouble in stopping the pitch rate completely at this point, so you may like to practice this little maneouvre two or three times before we get onto the roll proper. Once we are able to arrest the pitch cleanly and without jerking the aeroplane, all we then do is to apply full aileron (in either direction), and keep the elevators and rudder quite still. The aeroplane will then fly itself around the roll, and will finish in a shallow dive. As soon as the wings reach the level position, centralise the ailerons, and smoothly pull out.

We can now see that a roll of sorts can be made without using elevators or rudder, under control, without effort. However, it bore little resemblance to a slow roll, so having practiced it' a few more times, in both directions, we are ready to progress further. At this stage it is important to practice left and right rolls, so that one does not become "handed".

We repeat the manoeuvre until we reach the inverted position, but now we centralise the ailerons in order to maintain steady inverted flight. We can see the horizon, the only difference being that it is upside down; the control movements to move the nose up or down in relation to the horizon are just the same as when we were erect. The correct position for level inverted flight is with the leading edge of the top wing in line with the horizon as seen from the rear cockpit, and we make very gentle corrections with the elevator to keep it there. We have not yet used the rudder at all, and the ailerons are used naturally to keep the wings parallel with the horizon. This is "key point B". If we call our initial starting position in a 20° climb "key point A", we now have two reference points which we must achieve in the slow roll. I call them "key points" because they are the key to the whole manoeuvre.

To return to our student, who is still inverted. We can practice letting the nose go above and below the horizon, and then returning it to key point "B" with the elevators, until we are quite familiar with it. before going on to the second half of the slow roll.

We now press forward on the stick very slightly and at the same time smoothly apply aileron, maintaining the slight forward stick pressure. What you are doing here is pushing the aeroplane's nose above the horizon, and as the bank increases, this small amount of forward pressure will cause the nose to move to one side of the cloud at which we have been pointing. As the wings reach the vertical position we release the slight push force, and instead, we press backwards very slightly on the stick. At the same time, we press gentle rudder, in the same direction as the ailerons, i.e. if the stick is to the right, use right rudder.

As the aeroplane approaches level·flight again, you will notice that the roll is trying to speed up: this is because of the rudder you have just applied, so to maintain the same rate of roll, the amount of aileron must be reduced a little. Also you will notice that the aeroplane is sideslipping, due to the rudder, and this is quite correct. Do not expect the ball to be in the middle during a slow roll. You will also observe that the nose has swung a little across the horizon and is now once again pointing at the cloud. If we had not pushed forward a little on the stick as we left the inverted position, that swing would have caused us to lose direction. Do not, therefore, struggle to hold the nose on a point by means of harsh rudder in the last quarter of the roll, because you will induce so much sideslip that you will fall out of the manoeuvre. Rather, try to think of the rudder as a means of "putting the brakes on" the rate at which the nose is falling. Excess rudder will also reduce elevator authority (due to blanking), thus requiring more back stick. We have now flown two separate halves of a slow roll, and we repeat this, in both directions, always making sure that we achieve both key points. Soon, we are ready to progress further, and we do this gradually by reducing the time spent in inverted flight until eventually the whole roll is continuous. We must beware of reaching the inverted position with the nose too low, at which point things could get a little out of hand. In particular, if the nose drops, we must never pull through in the second half of a loop; the speed will be too high, and we would lose an enormous amount of height. This is what "key point B" is for: if you ever reach the inverted position with the nose low, stop the roll, and push the nose back to key point "B", then continue normally. Learning the roll in two halves does two other things; it allows the student time to think and prepare himself for the next phase, and it gets rid of the natural tendency for the roll to stop apparently of its own accord at the inverted position. This occurs because some psychological factor makes the student release the aileron pressure when he is upside down, perhaps because he is thinking about elevators or even rudder!

Now we are able to fly a passable slow roll, but actually we are still rolling quite quickly, although we are now maintaining both height and direction, and from the ground it will look quite presentable.

Here we encounter a small problem; although we are doing exactly the same as before, now that we are rolling more slowly

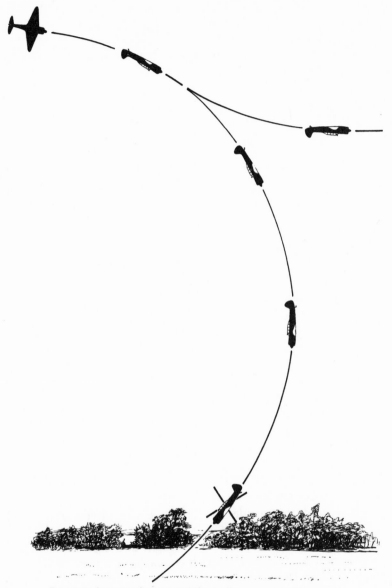

Recovery from poorly executed slow roll — correct and incorrect

we notice that the nose is swinging off heading and going below the horizon as we approach the inverted position; it is only the fact that we remember to achieve key point "B" by stopping the roll that prevents us from losing a lot of height; but at least we now know that we can recover by this method.

What is happening is this; when we started the manoeuvre at key point "A", we initially rolled quite quickly, using full aileron, and although the nose started to drop, we had reached key point "B" before it fell below the horizon. Now, with the slower roll rate, this is no longer the case: something, therefore, must be done. We must bring in the rudder. Once again we achieve key point "A", and start rolling, more slowly this time. As the wings approach the vertically banked position, we can see the nose starting to drop. We do not try and stop this completely, but once again use the rudder as a "brake", to retard the downward progress of the nose when the aeroplane is on its side. In this case the rudder is gently applied in the opposite direction to the ailerons; it will be appreciated that the controls are now almost the same as for a sideslip, and if too much rudder is used, with insufficiently powerful ailerons, the roll could stop! The amount of rudder used here will depend on the airspeed, the rate of roll, and the starting angle (key point "A"). If one has misjudged the angle, and started with the nose too low, or rolled too slowly, or with the airspeed too low, or even done all these, there may not be enough rudder to prevent the nose from falling below the horizon.

As we approach the inverted position, we start to press forward on the stick; it is more pressure than actual movement, and I use the phrase "accept the weight of the aeroplane".

If this is done too soon, perhaps because the nose is too low, again we will see this unwanted swing away from the point at which we are aiming. The rudder is still deflected in the opposite direction to the roll as we reach key point "B" so we can see that the controls are "crossed".

Because most aircraft have differential ailerons, when inverted, the aileron drag is very high, and is made worse by the high angle of attack necessary in inverted flight. In order to keep straight we must hold this rudder on until we have left the inverted position, at which point the rudder is slowly released, reaching neutral with just over 90° of roll to go, and continuing in the same direction as aileron in the last quarter of the roll.

One word of caution: if the airspeed is low, and the rate of roll too slow as the aircraft reaches the inverted position, it will be remembered that the controls are well and truly crossed. If at the same time the nose is a little too low and one uses too much forward stick pressure to try and reach key point "B", one realises that the aircraft is now set up for an inverted flick roll, and it is

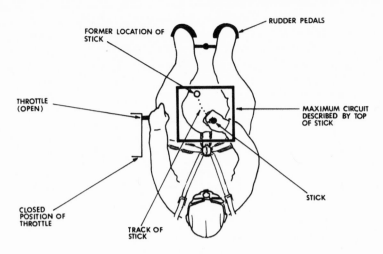

Key to slow roll drawing

a little too early in the syllabus for these! The Stampe has a great tendency to flick here if the front cockpit is open and unoccupied; so for all solo flying the metal cover should be fitted and the windscreen removed from that cockpit. When this is done, make sure all front seat straps are secured.

The final touch to the slow roll is achieved when, (instead of lifting the nose to key point "A") with the bank coming on, from level flight, opposite rudder is used to skid the nose upwards in the first quarter, after which the same rudder pressure will control the rate at which the nose comes down, as the airspeed falls. During this phase, the aircraft has a very slight tendency to pitch forward, which may be contained by a little backwards pressure on the stick. With the engine running at full throttle throughout, the exact amount of rudder will differ depending on the roll direction, due to slipstream effects, as well as for the factors previously mentioned.

Slow Roll

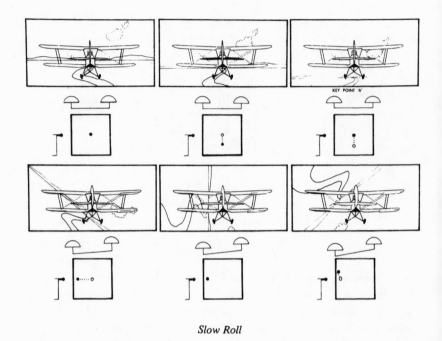

Slow Roll

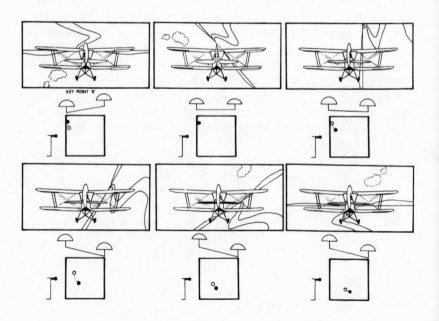

Some machines will roll better in one direction; usually rigging plays a more important part than engine rotation, except in vertical rolls, which will be covered later.

If one progresses in stages, as described here, one can thoroughly master one aspect of the roll before going on to the next. At the same time it will allow the student to execute the roll safely in the early stages, and he can then progress just as fast as he wants to. He can develop his own style, because this is what aerobatics are all about. The slow roll is really the key to advanced aerobatics.

7   The basic manoeuvres - the stall turn

With our repertoire limited to loops and rolls, we are restricted in that we cannot turn around! It follows that if we are ever going to be able to construct and fly an aerobatic sequence, we are going to have to have a wide selection of turn-round manoeuvres available. The most useful of these is the stall turn, which, although it has many hundreds of combinations, we shall consider here in its basic form.

It differs, too, from loops and rolls, in that the timing is much more critical. With the first two manoeuvres we experienced a reasonable degree of latitude in their execution, which, although it might have made the manoeuvre appear slightly different, was still acceptable. The entry and exit of the stall turn conform to this trend, but the actual "turn" is critical, and there is only one moment when one can do this if it is to approach perfection.

It is also the first manoeuvre where we have a sustained vertical flight path, both up and down; and it is vital that the lessons we learn here are well learned, as they will provide the foundation for advanced vertical work later. Because we will be pointing vertically upwards, with very little forward speed, we should remember the exercises in recovery from this position, together with the action to be taken in the event of an accidental tailslide.

The purpose of the stall turn in its basic form is to reverse direction. It accomplishes this by establishing a vertical climb until the aeroplane is almost stationary. It then cartwheels to the left or right, through 180°, until it is pointing vertically downwards, following which it regains level flight, but is now travelling in the opposite direction. The vertical climb and its entry, and the vertical dive and its exit are accomplished with the elevator, using the ailerons and rudder to maintain direction. The actual yawed turn at the top is made with rudder, which may or may not be assisted by the engine. During this phase, the ailerons are used to maintain the plane of the cartwheel, and the elevators are held in the neutral position, except that they can be used in conjunction with the engine to assist the rudder.

Once again we trim the aeroplane for aerobatics and accelerate with the wings level and the slip ball in the centre. With 100 knots on the ASI, we establish level flight, preferably into wind above a suitable axis, such as a railway line. Since there is a chance that the propeller may stop, we had better make sure that there is a suitable field within gliding distance; it is a most depressing sensation, gliding silently earthwards, trying to pick a decent landing area, if one has not had the forethought to select one beforehand! We pick a good field alongside our railway line, so now we are ready to begin. One hundred knots is quite fast enough, but if we have trouble in establishing the vertical we can use 120 knots.

The first part of the manoeuvre is very much like the first quarter of the loop, but it is pulled much tighter, using full power. As we reach 70° of pitch, we look at each wingtip in turn and keep each of them at the same level relative to the horizon: this is most important. The pitch continues at the same high rate until the wings appear to be vertical with respect to the horizon at which point the elevators are returned to neutral, so that the vertical climb is maintained. In the early stages it does not matter if the pitch angle is short of the vertical; but do not get "onto your back", i.e. just beyond the vertical. The fuselage, of course, will not be vertical due to the angle of incidence at which the wings are attached, and this situation is deliberate, in order to make sure that the aircraft is not over the vertical.

It is essential that the pull up was straight, otherwise one wing might be slightly low. As the speed falls, the elevators are used to ensure that the correct pitch attitude is maintained, but due to propeller effects the nose will start to yaw to the right (propeller turning anti-clockwise as seen from the cockpit).

This will be seen as a tendency for the left wing to be higher than the right wing against the horizon, and it must be corrected with left rudder, applied progressively. When we have applied about one quarter left rudder (engine still at full power), the speed will be falling through about 40 knots. This is the moment we have been waiting for! Smoothly but quickly we push on full right rudder, and the aircraft responds by cartwheeling to the right through 180°, still with full power on. If it is done properly there will be no need to use ailerons or elevators. About 10° before the vertical diving position, we use left rudder as a "brake" to prevent the nose from swinging through the vertical. The aircraft, still with very little speed, tends to behave like a pendulum, and the rudder must be used to stop this from occurring, and to make sure that the nose points straight down. As we use rudder in this way we notice that the aeroplane is trying to "tuck under" slightly, so we press backwards on the stick sufficiently to prevent this from happening. Really, all we are doing is to use all the controls as necessary to point that nose absolutely straight down. At this point there is a great tendency to pull back hard on the stick; after all, are we not pointing straight at terra firma, and with full power on, at that? However, we must resist the temptation; first because the speed is still very low and it would be only too easy to stall

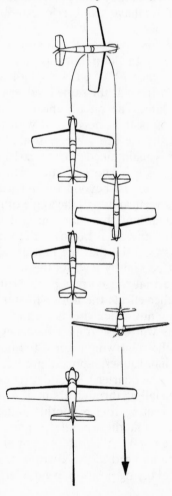

Stall Turn

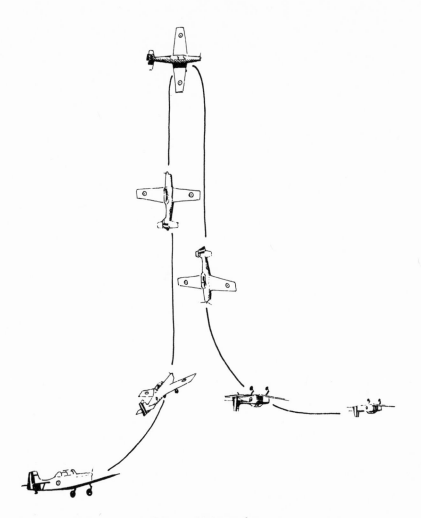

Stall Turn with inverted recovery

and flick, and secondly because we want to preserve the shape of
the manoeuvre. If we went up 300 feet, we must come down 300
feet, and so on. So many pilots fly a faultless stall turn, and then
spoil the whole thing by pulling out early. Try to remember to
leave the aeroplane pointing straight down for one to two seconds
before pulling out. By this time, with full power on, the speed
should be increasing nicely, so that a crisp pull into level flight not
only marks the end of the manoeuvre, but also results in a speed
of 100 knots ready for the next figure.

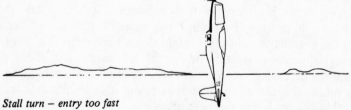

Stall turn – entry too fast

One of the most common faults with the stall turn is the inability to find the vertical quickly and accurately, and since this is going to be a primary requirement in the future it might be as well to get it sorted out now. We can therefore just practice achieving the vertical without actually stall turning, pausing to have a good look at the angle we have actually attained, before practising our "recovery from the vertical". With the vertical climb mastered, the "turn" may present a few problems. Because we are understandably concerned about tailsliding, the initial tendency will be to put on the rudder too soon. This will result in the aeroplane skidding upwards sideways, instead of pivoting neatly about its CG. Remembering our "secondary effects of controls" we will not be unduly surprised to find that the aeroplane starts to roll in the same direction as the rudder; indeed it may even roll to the inverted position!

During the upward skid there is quite a lot of drag and also the natural stability of the aeroplane opposes the excess rudder we have applied. These two effects neutralise each other with the result that all the yaw stops, with the nose still above the horizon, and shortly afterwards the aeroplane stops too. This marvellous demonstration of levitation is usually short-lived, and the aeroplane then falls out of the sky, to the mortification of the pilot.

One can, however, prevent the collapse of the manoeuvre, even after one has put the rudder on too soon. If any roll develops, it follows that there must be a sufficient airflow remaining for this to occur. That being so, the ailerons will still be functional, and should be used as necessary to neutralise the roll. If the yaw stops with the nose above the horizon, the inclined thrust vector is helping to keep it there; so, close the throttle and the nose will drop. The unwanted roll can also be caused by being "over" the vertical. In all of this we are ignoring the effect of wind on the flightpath; this will be considered later.

If the application of rudder is left too late, apart from the possibility of tailsliding, it is probable that the aeroplane will fall forwards and sideways; the only real cure is to use rudder sooner.

If the rudder does not have the desired effect, it is possible that the aircraft is inclined away from the required direction of stall turn, i.e. left wing down, and wanting to go right. Alternatively, because of corrections in the vertical climb, the aircraft may be in a vertical sideslip condition, which means that it can only be stall turned with the sideslip.

So far we have only discussed a stall turn "with" the engine; now it is time to consider a stall turn "against" the engine, i.e. to the left in the Stampe.

We use precisely the same technique, except that we apply the rudder as the speed falls through 50 knots, and we apply about half rudder quite smartly, at the same time throttling back to half power. As the aircraft starts to yaw, we steadily push on the rest of the rudder and simultaneously throttle smoothly back, so that as the nose cuts through the horizon, we achieve full rudder and a closed throttle at the same instant.

If this is not timed exactly, the yaw will stop, with the nose up, as described previously. If this happens, and the yaw begins to slow down, pull the stick back sharply; this will utilise the gyroscopic properties of the engine and propeller and will increase the yaw. If this is not enough, throttle back, as indicated earlier.

On some aeroplanes, which have a large and powerful engine, and a short fuselage and span; if the power is left on during the stall turn "with" the engine, the aircraft will roll uncontrollably. On these machines, the throttle will have to be retarded no matter which direction the stall turn. Additionally, when the machine is pointing straight down, it is necessary to wait until there is enough airspeed for good aileron control before opening the throttle, or the aircraft may torque roll in the dive.

Some short coupled aeroplanes with a large keel area in front of the CG are difficult to stall turn cleanly, and for these a special technique is necessary.

Earlier we saw that if there was any inadvertent sideslip in the vertical climb it could prove impossible to stall turn against it. It follows therefore that if we deliberately sideslip in the required direction the aeroplane has no choice except to stall turn as directed. How then, are we to produce a vertical sideslip, because if we start fooling around with aileron and rudder, will we not only lose our vertical line, but perhaps even start rolling as well?

Once again, we find the explanation is quite simple: the sideslip is set up before we begin the manoeuvre. Let us assume we wish to stall turn to the left. Having settled the aeroplane down in level flight, we apply a touch of left aileron to give us no more than 2° bank, and at the same time keep straight with right rudder. If your aeroplane has any dihedral the judges may not notice this 2°. Just before pulling up, level the wings so that the pull-up is straight, although the aeroplane is still carrying right rudder and is slipping to the left. From the ground it will appear to be straight and square. The sideslip will persist up to the moment when the rudder is reversed and the result will be a positive rate of yaw in the required direction. It is more important to consider the use of the vertical sideslip when stall turning "against" the engine. The more rudder travel one has available at the moment of stall turning, the better and cleaner will be the manoeuvre. It then follows that if one arrives at the top of the vertical climb holding half right rudder in readiness for a left stall turn, or vice versa, the manoeuvre will be cleaner than if the rudder were neutral, because one is using three-quarters of the total rudder sweep to power the manoeuvre, instead of only half.

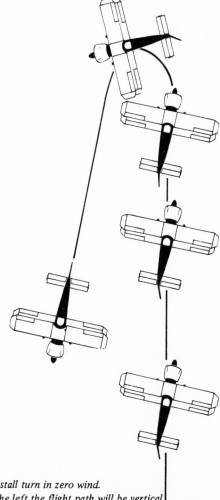

Vertical Side Slip with stall turn in zero wind.
N.B. With wind from the left the flight path will be vertical

At first, the results of our stall turn attempts will have the appearance of a slight "fly-around" manoeuvre, where one is actually describing the arc of a circle. This is caused by applying the rudder too soon, and can be identified from inside the aeroplane by the need to "hold off" aileron. In the perfect stall turn the aeroplane pivots on its CG. However, as long as the centre point of the rotation is inside the wing span, it is generally considered acceptable.

Now that we can fly the four basic figures: loop, roll, spin and stall turn, we are able to combine these manoeuvres and enlarge our repertoire. There is no limit to what can be achieved.

8 *Basic combination manoeuvres*

The basic elements of the loop, roll and stall turn have been gone into in some detail because they are the basis of all flown manoeuvres. The aeroplane has freedom of movement in three axes, and we can now fly one manoeuvre based on each axis; therefore it follows that by combining these basic figures, we can start to learn more advanced manoeuvres. The other type of figure is the autorotative figure, which we know from the spin, where the machine rotates about all three axes simultaneously.

We are approaching the point where we can consider building a sequence, but before we do this we have to consider that in all our flying so far we have contrived to lose height, if only in the dive to gain speed for a manoeuvre. Obviously what is required is a figure which will regain some altitude.

Roll-off-the-top
To give it the full description, it is a half roll off the top of a half loop. Sometimes wrongly referred to as an Immelman turn, it provides a height gain in addition to a reversal of direction; so now we have another method of turning round.

Referring back to our speed formula, we remember that this figure requires three times the stalling speed to begin, i.e. 120 knots, which also coincides with maximum rpm at full throttle.

Having trimmed the aeroplane, we accelerate in level flight so as not to waste valuable height. When we have reached maximum level speed, we lower the nose to accelerate to 120 knots, whereupon we check level momentarily with wings level and ball in the centre. We commence the manoeuvre as in a loop, but we must pull tighter because we need sufficient speed at the top to be able to half roll out. This is also why we needed 120 knots to begin.

Instead of relaxing the pressure as we pass the vertical, we keep pulling, until, throwing our heads back, we can see the inverted horizon. The pitch rate is still quite fast, and just before we reach key point "B" of the slow roll, we release all the back pressure on the stick, and simultaneously apply full aileron. Our speed is very

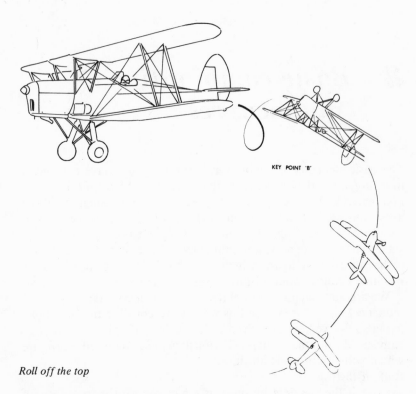

KEY POINT 'B'

Roll off the top

low, so we will need maximum aileron to give us a decent rate of roll; also, because of the low speed, we have the nose just a touch higher than key point "B". As we apply the aileron, we press forward gently on the stick as we did in the slow roll, and for the same reason. The rudder, all this time, has been neutral, but as the wings pass the vertically banked position we start applying rudder in the direction of roll, just as we did in the slow roll. We must remember that because the speed is low, the nose must be held higher to maintain level flight, and we recall our straight and level revision, flying at different airspeeds. We note that we have gained over 300 feet in this manoeuvre, as we accelerate away, still at full power.

Having already learned the loop and roll, there is not much to go wrong here, but there are one or two problem areas. In the first place, one is not yet used to the higher values of *g* encountered in this manoeuvre, so one can tire very quickly. Again, rather than struggle on and on, if it's not working properly, land, and have a rest, before trying again.

A common fault is not to release the back pressure completely before starting the roll, whereupon one tends to finish up in a turn as the wings reach the vertical. Any tendency for a persistent heading error in the manoeuvre could well be due to this. Another tendency is to apply rudder too soon and too hard, thus yawing the nose up into the air, whereupon everything tends to stop, including the propeller. When I learned this manoeuvre on a Tiger Moth, I stopped the engine three times in one day, doing just this. Luckily for me, it started in the dive each time!

Because of the low airspeed in the roll, the direction of engine rotation is now of greater importance, and will result in the roll-off-the-top to the right being easier than to the left. Indeed, when rolling left, one can finish up with full rudder applied, and with the nose still dragging to the right. The amount of rudder needed is dependent on the airspeed and amount of power being used. There is a great temptation here to only do rolls off to the right, but this should be resisted; if one is to achieve a high standard, all handed manoeuvres must be flown both ways. If one is a little slow in the roll off to the left, there are two methods of correction available. The first is to allow the nose to fall below the horizon, whilst still keeping it straight; having given up the level fly-off, one can now use the extra control to keep direction constant, and as soon as the wings are level, the nose can be lifted to the correct altitude. The second method is to throttle back slightly, which will reduce the adverse turning moment from the propeller. However, it will also reduce thrust and direct lift, and may cause the aircraft to stall. One can use any combination of these two, depending on circumstances. If one is flying on the B axis, towards or away from the judges, they are not going to see any sink as easily as if the aircraft were on the main axis, therefore in this case it might be better to stay at full power and drop the nose a little. An obvious solution might be thought to be acceptable which involves delaying between the half loop and the half roll to allow the aeroplane to accelerate, but this would constitute two separate figures. In this manoeuvre we want to see the pitching energy changed instantaneously into rolling energy, with no discernible pause in between. If we start at the correct speed and pull just the right amount of g for that speed, we will reach the top of the loop with the maximum possible airspeed, from which we can fly our half roll cleanly, without having to use large bootfuls of rudder, which will produce noticeable sideslip and will look clumsy and ugly. Remember, the higher the airspeed at the top of the loop, the less rudder will be required in the roll. Another method of improving directional control in the roll-off is to use just a trace of opposite rudder when starting the roll, as we found was necessary to a greater extent in the slow roll, to eliminate aileron drag with its unwanted turning effects. Only a very small amount of rudder is required here; if there are any problems, it is better to go back to the basic method and lock the rudder during the early part of the roll. Always remember that misuse of the rudder causes nearly all the minor problems in aerobatics; if in doubt, use less, rather than more. Excess rudder in the latter stages of the roll-off-the-top will cause a lateral displacement of the aeroplane, in an attempt to keep the nose on the correct point, when the error was really in not pushing the nose to one side with forward stick, when the aircraft was vertically banked, as we saw in the slow roll. Many pilots tend to forget that the second half of the roll-off is the same as the second half of a slow roll, albeit at a lower airspeed.

Cuban 8
Having learned the roll-off-the-top, the next obvious step is to progress to the Cuban 8, since it is very similar in its execution, and can be used not only as a combination figure in its complete form, but as a turn-round manoeuvre if one completes only half of the figure. The complete Cuban 8 traces out the pattern of a figure of eight lying on its side, where the aircraft carries out five-eighths of a loop, pausing in an inverted 45° dive, and then half rolling on that line before pulling out. One has now flown half the manoeuvre, so that by repeating the sequence immediately one can complete the full figure 8.

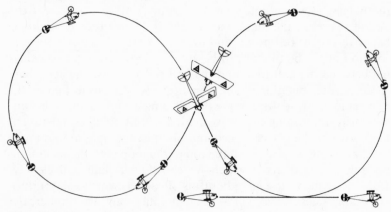

Cuban Eight

Since the half roll takes place in the dive, where the aircraft is accelerating, it is not necessary to use the same speed as for the roll-off: 100 knots will be quite sufficient. Here we will consider half the manoeuvre in detail, since this is the form most commonly used in the more advanced competitions. We will also learn the technique of linking the two halves to form a symmetric figure.

Again we ensure that the aeroplane is trimmed slightly nose heavy, and we check momentarily in level flight with the slip ball centred, at 100 knots. Using full power, we press back on the stick, and fly the first half of a loop in exactly the same way as if we really were going to loop. As the nose comes down gently through the horizon, we are making a conscious effort to "round off" the top of the manoeuvre, as we did in the loop, but as the nose comes down to the 45° inverted dive position, instead of continuing the loop, we now release all the back pressure, so that the aircraft holds the 45° line, and here our "nose heavy" trim helps us. If we can now imagine a new key point "C", which is half-way between the nose cowling and the top wing, looking straight ahead through the windscreen, this is the spot around which we are going to roll. If we are lucky it will coincide with a point on the ground, perhaps a road bridge across the railway that we are using as our main axis. An imaginary line drawn from your eyes to that spot on the ground is the line around which the aeroplane is going to roll. As in all loop-roll combinations, we must make sure that all the elevator deflection has been cancelled, otherwise the machine will go off heading. As we start to roll, we again push the nose a shade up and to one side as the wings approach the vertical position, and with just under 90° left to roll, we apply gentle rudder in the direction of roll: just enough to allow the aircraft to point once again at key point "C". Now we are in an erect 45° dive, which we hold just long enough to balance the shape of the manoeuvre, before pulling out crisply, but without snatching the stick, into level flight. We will find that the speed will be slightly higher than entry speed, and the exit height may be a little lower, but we have now accomplished another turn-round figure, and now we have speed to immediately commence another manoeuvre.

Should we wish to complete the Cuban 8, we would not have held the dive line quite so long after the half roll. Instead we would have started a gentle pull out with the pitch rate reaching its maximum at the bottom of the dive, this pitch rate then leading into the next half Cuban 8. At this point, the speed and height should be the same as during the original entry; this being the main difference in the full manoeuvre. The primary intention is to visualise a perfect 8 shape in the sky, and to try and fly it. Again this figure should be practised to the right and left; in fact it is a good idea to incorporate both roll directions in each full Cuban 8. in practice. Although the manoeuvre should be easier to fly than the roll-off-the-top, one very often finds minor problems in the early stages, probably because this manoeuvre goes on for quite a long time, and also because the student can see the ground approaching rapidly while he is rolling with the nose down, and the natural tendency is to get it over with quickly! The big secret here is, very simply, don't rush it – after all, we have plenty of speed and control. Occasionally a student will lose direction during the pull up into the looping half of the manoeuvre because he is already thinking about the roll. There is no reason why one should sacrifice a simple half loop; just attend to one thing at a time, so that with a perfect half loop behind us, we can now concentrate on rolling.

There is also a tendency to get on with it, which results in the aeroplane being pulled too quickly over the top of the loop, which then has a distinct "peak". Inevitably this is because the student is worried about the airspeed building up too fast in the half roll. Another result of this worry is that the line before and after the half roll is usually more like 25°, and this especially applies to the second line. By this stage the student is in a state of despair, because if he tries to achieve 45° the speed gets out of hand, and a reason for this is that he is often reluctant to use full aileron initially. Remember that the speed is low when the roll starts so full aileron is required; it should then be reduced as the speed builds up to maintain a constant roll rate. If he has not pushed the nose upwards slightly and to one side in the half roll he will see the nose sliding sideways away from key point "C", and he will probably not be able to resist using too much rudder, too early, which will look terrible!

However, be on guard against pushing forward too much, as the aircraft will then have a distinct "barrelling" tendency, which is very noticeable from the ground. As in the roll-offs we can use a trace of opposite rudder as we apply aileron to offset the aileron drag and its unwanted turning moment, but it is better in the early stages to leave the rudder absolutely alone until we have passed the wings vertical position, and then use it gently and sparingly to maintain direction. The key to success is to co-ordinate the control inputs so that the aircraft rolls exactly around key point "C". Keep your eyes glued onto that point during the roll.

A variation of technique is to co-ordinate the end of the looping phase with the beginning of the rolling phase so that the transition takes place between the top of the loop and the 45° diving line, but this type of manoeuvre would not score very well in a competition, although it makes a good co-ordination exercise.

If one persistently has trouble in maintaining height, perhaps because of a particularly slow rate of roll on certain types of aeroplane, a solution here is to increase the starting speed. You will still lose height, but it will be in the initial dive, and not in the manoeuvre, because the higher speed will give a bigger loop, and thus allow a longer 45° line with more time to roll. The two most common faults are: difficulty in achieving and maintaining the exact 45° line, and misuse of rudder in the roll. The 45° line will play a very important part in more advanced figures later so it is vital that one learns exactly what it looks like, both erect and inverted, and one will find that if one gets out of practice, the 45° line is the first thing to suffer.

Many pilots draw or paint lines on their windscreens or canopies to mark the 45° lines, up and down. This is a bit of a waste of time, because the line is only good for one speed, one aircraft weight, in zero wind, and at a given height, because in the lower levels, the apparent height of the horizon changes. Eventually you will get used to making these pitch corrections as conditions change; do not become rigidly locked to a painted line. In the end, it is practice alone that will produce perfection.

Reverse Cuban 8

Having learned the normal Cuban 8, a natural follow-on is to learn the reverse Cuban 8, which, as its name implies, is merely a reversal of the previous figure. Once again it describes a figure 8 lying on its side, and it is achieved by executing a climbing half roll at 45°, followed by a downward five-eighths loop into level flight. The sequence is then repeated to give the complete figure, though it will be obvious that if one flies only half of the manoeuvre another turn-round figure will have been added to our repertoire.

To select the starting speed, since the roll is really halfway between a horizontal and vertical roll, we average out the speed required, i.e. 110 knots, in our Stampe. This should result in no height loss if we fly it properly, but by using a higher entry speed we can fly a bigger figure and come out higher up. Since you never get anything for nothing in aerobatics, height must be sacrificed in the first place by diving to get speed.

Having clearly marked our entry in balanced flight, we pull up quite sharply, but again without snatching, to 45°. You should not pull any more than about 4g at this point. The line is established, clearly and confidently, and the pitch rate checked, without overcontrolling. This 45° line must be achieved instantly without overcorrecting or otherwise wasting time, because the airspeed will by now be falling rapidly. At this early stage, do not attempt to slow roll in the climb, but going back to the technique we used to learn the slow roll, lock the rudder, and roll quite quickly. As the aeroplane approaches the inverted position, accept the weight inverted, with slight forward stick pressure. As this is done, because we are still in the final stages of rolling as the stick is pressed forward, we will need a touch of opposite rudder to oppose aileron drag, remembering that differential ailerons are very definitely non-differential when we are in inverted flight. As the roll stops, and we must beware of the tendency to roll too far, we notice that with the rapidly decreasing air speed there is a tendency for the nose to go much further up than we want it to, so not only must we virtually release all forward pressure on the stick, but because of our nose heavy trim we may even have to press back a little to stop the attitude from getting too steep. We keep one eye on the airspeed, and we start to pull gently, very gently, around the top of the loop, when the speed has fallen to 65 knots. During the pull-round, the speed will probably fall off the clock, but we are not concerned because we are now used to the idea that only angle of attack matters.

We use ailerons and rudder to keep straight, and as we come over the top, we can pick up our feature line. We may notice that we are carrying almost full right rudder, but the aeroplane is running straight: we have done this instinctively. It is only when we consider the slipstream and gyroscopic effects that we realise why all this rudder is needed; but we must never, never, just push the rudder on at that point. This would be simply flying by numbers, and we remember that misuse of rudder is the biggest adverse factor against flying good aerobatics.

The aeroplane is merely flown gently over the top of the loop, using all controls to make it go where we want it to, regardless of the position of the controls themselves. As we reach the inverted position with the nose going down through the horizon,

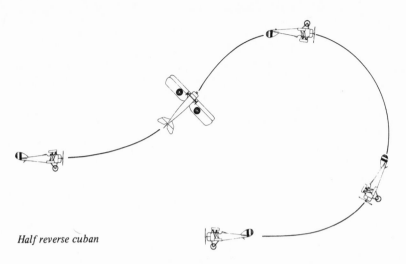

Half reverse cuban

still using full power, all we have to do is to finish the loop, as we have done before. Be careful here, because we have been sitting quite relaxed under negative g, and we are now going to pull about $+4g$, so take a deep breath on the way down and brace against the rising acceleration. Your g threshold is always very much lower after a period of negative g. Take care, too, as in the loop, not to stall in the pull round.

At the bottom, we can either establish our horizontal line to mark the end of a half reverse Cuban 8, or we can continue the pull to 45°, and repeat for the complete manoeuvre.

Again this figure should be flown both left and right, and here we will encounter marked slipstream effects.

If we roll "with" the engine, i.e. to the right with our Stampe, we will need left rudder when we reach the inverted position because we are now sideslipping as a result of the roll. At the same time we need right rudder to compensate for propeller effects now that we are inverted, for the same reasons that we need left rudder on take-off and in the erect climb.

These two effects counteract each other to a large extent, so that we hardly need any rudder at all in practice, after the roll. However, if we roll "against" the engine, i.e. left, the rudder effects are now additive, and we will need considerable right rudder to keep straight. This will obviously cause extra drag and so reduce performance, so in a competition we would normally roll only to the right. We must still practice left rolls, though, if only to be able to roll Lycoming engined aeroplanes!

So if you find yourself using a lot of rudder, and everything else looks O.K., don't necessarily think you've got it wrong, but at the same time don't just shove on rudder as a matter of course.

The biggest problem in this manoeuvre is in attaining and holding the 45° climb with a straight line of equal length both before and after the roll. Sometimes the line is shallow, so that the downward loop is entered at an excessive speed with the attendant serious height loss and high *g*, producing a danger of blackout; or alternatively the line is allowed to steepen until the angle is nearer 70° which usually results in the aircraft falling out of the top of the manoeuvre. Whatever happens, remember that if you have the stick back, the spin, if it occurs, will be erect, and not inverted.

To some extent, the tendency for the attitude of the aircraft to steepen is beneficial, because, as the speed falls, we will need a greater angle of attack to provide the same amount of lift, in order to maintain a 45° flightpath. Since it is flightpath which the judges are going to mark in the competition it is as well to get used to achieving this right from the beginning. But be careful not to hold the line too long, and this is one reason for pulling down from not less than 65 knots. The art is to know the exact amount of compromise.

9 *Basic sequences*

Now that we are able to fly a good cross section of basic figures, we can think about joining them together to make a sequence. Indeed we have already begun to do so in a small way if we consider the two halves of a Cuban 8 as separate manoeuvres. Let us first consider the reaons for wanting to design and fly a sequence. We may just want to fly a continuous series of manoeuvres to impress our passenger, or to amuse ourselves, and if we are really out to demonstrate skill, we would want to give our innocent passenger the smoothest ride possible. On the other hand, if our audience is on the ground, be it an airshow crowd or a panel of judges, we are going to demonstrate clean, smooth, precision flying.

Of the two styles, the latter is the more difficult, because one has to keep the aeroplane in a very small area of sky, and it is to this end that we are working. On many occasions I have watched an inexperienced competitor drifting away downwind, oblivious to his position, but obviously totally engrossed in following his sequence. Here again, sequence design can be at fault, in that some sequences hold well in a strong wind, and some do not. It is as well to start by drawing a sequence that ought to maintain its position in a wind, although we will not initially be trying to stay over one spot; it will at least get us used to the philosophy. The wind direction is usually drawn in, and it is customary for the first manoeuvre to start into wind, although, obviously, eventually we will be able to start in any direction.

We are therefore going to draw our sequence on a card which we will attach to the instrument panel for reference. This is not really necessary at this stage, but it is a good idea to get used to seeing the manoeuvre card there, and to be able to refer to it from time to time during the sequence. Because there is not much space on the instrument panel we need some form of shorthand to depict the various manoeuvres. and the method in current use throughout the entire world is the Aresti system. This will be described more fully later; for the moment it will suffice to learn the symbols for our basic manoeuvres.

Preparation and thinking on the ground is the key to success in the air. To present our sequence we must ensure a good balance between successive manoeuvres, and we must ensure that the exit speed from one manoeuvre is the correct entry speed for the next, without having to waste time by diving to gain speed. It becomes obvious, that at our present stage of learning, we would not start with a roll-off-the-top followed by a loop, because we would not have the required entry speed for the second figure.

It may help at this point to buy or construct a small model aeroplane, with which one can "fly" the sequence at home. It is quite remarkable that if one moves the aeroplane through the air at the correct relative speed, one finds that the average living room carpet is just about the right size for the real area used by the real aeroplane. Later on, when we come to fly sequences within the prescribed area, we will find that if the walls of the living room get in the way when "flying" the model, the real aeroplane will go out of the "box". By using the model, one can get an idea of what the sequence will look like, and one can also simulate the effects of wind drift with a little practice. If I can "fly "my model successfully indoors, I know without doubt that I can do it in the aeroplane. Also, we can simulate high or low performance aircraft quite realistically with a little practice.

Since the first manoeuvre we learned was a loop, let us start with that. We hold our model over the middle of the carpet and "fly" it around a loop. Excellent – full marks! Wouldn't it be great if the real thing worked out as well! For basic sequences, the philosophy is to make every other manoeuvre a central figure, starting with the first, so that the third, fifth and so on will be on centre. Next, we have a stall turn to the right, and now we come back for a slow roll to the right, "downwind". We find that the model will naturally stay central in the room, and we know that

the aircraft will do likewise in the air. Three figures will be enough to start with, as we will find that the extra thought processes involved at this stage will saturate the brain completely with the result that the individual manoeuvres suffer. The reasons for flying these three manoeuvres in this order will quickly become apparent when we realise that the loop, being into wind, will have its shape modified by that wind, which will round out the top, thus making things much easier. The stall turn, also into wind will have its flightpath steepened so that it will appear vertical.

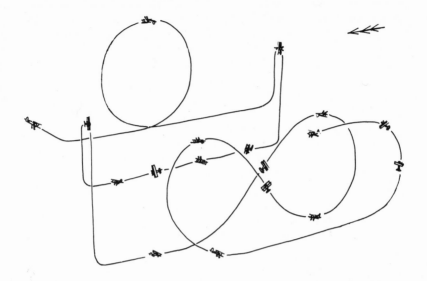

Typical sequence

The slow roll is downwind, which will make it look much more flowing and impressive, although of course it will very quickly go from one end of the "box" to the other.

Once we have got this far, we can now add to our basic sequence. As we exit from the slow roll right we are once again accelerating up to 100 knots, and we are also carrying some residual right rudder from the roll, causing a sideslip to the left. Why not do a stall turn to the left, using the sideslip to enable us to turn "against" the engine? Of course the wind is behind us, so our flightpath is not vertical, but otherwise it will fit. This will bring us back into wind for a Cuban 8, on centre, followed by a roll-off-the-top to the right to finish the sequence.

Although we have been aware of the wind direction and the effects of it, we have not specifically been trying to stay over a point. In fact, if we had paid more attention to our position we would have been agreeably surprised to find that we have not moved very far, We have been mainly concerned about maintaining direction, and because of the attention to detail in the individual figures learned previously, there should have been no problem here.

Try and remember how much height was lost, not only in the entire sequence, but in each individual manoeuvre because this will assume more importance as we get lower.

As the flying becomes more advanced, the aeroplane is working harder, so stay alert for any unusual noise or vibration, and keep a careful eye on the engine instruments. Don't get carried away, quite literally, especially in a strong wind. Remember which way you have to go to get home, and always carry a map.

10 *Inverted flying and turns*

Since it is possible to double one's repertoire by flying all one's manoeuvres upside down, one would expect that it would have been introduced at a much earlier stage. Although ordinary inverted straight and level flight is quite simple, the manoeuvres resulting from it are less so.

The flying up to this point has been practiced with a view to improving co-ordination and accuracy, and it has also resulted in increased confidence in the strength of the machine and the ability to control it. A very large amount of one's future flying will depend upon being able to fly inverted as well as one does the right way up, so the importance of inverted flying cannot be over emphasised.

Erect and inverted attitudes – ZLIN and Akrostar

In the case of a conventional wing, the lift coefficient in inverted flight is much lower, resulting in an increased stalling speed; and this means that the angle of attack must be higher during inverted flight to maintain height at a given speed. The angle of the fuselage when inverted if further exaggerated by the fact that the wing is usually attached at a positive angle of incidence. Only in the case of a specialist aerobatic aeroplane, with symmetrical wings attached to the fuselage at zero incidence, would the fuselage angle be the same inverted as erect, and in this case the inverted and erect stalling speeds would be the same.

Many students hold the mistaken belief that the controls are all "reversed" when the aircraft is inverted, and in this frame of mind it is small wonder that they get confused. As we saw in the preliminaries to the slow roll, steady inverted flight is a very straightforward affair. At the same time, the aircraft was designed to fly the right way up and to demonstrate a reasonable level of stability (specialist aerobatic aircraft excepted).

The more stable the machine in normal flight, the heavier it will be in inverted flight on the controls; for example, if the tail-plane is set at a high negative incidence on the fuselage, it will give strong longitudinal dihedral, and therefore a powerful restoring force in the event of a disturbance. This, coupled with a forward C.G. can make it very tiring to hold the push force required for inverted flight, and it may be impossible to trim it out. On aeroplanes of this sort, one has to use the trimmer to fly aerobatics, and this will not result in a good performance. Since most aerobatic machines have some positive longitudinal stability , there will always be a push force in inverted flight. By trimming nose heavy, we can compensate to some extent for this. In addition, most aircraft have dihedral, and this is provided to give lateral stability. It follows that the machine will be laterally unstable when inverted. Many aircraft have a fixed trim on the rudder, which in the case of the Stampe holds on a little left rudder, which allows the aircraft to fly straight when the pilot takes his feet off the rudder bar. When the aircraft is upside down, we need right rudder, as seen from inside, although an outside observer would still consider that the rudder was deflected to the left.

These are the reasons why the myth has grown that the controls are reversed. Many modern aerobatic aeroplanes have extremely low stability in pitch and roll, so that the inverted and erect handling is nearly the same, but these machines are difficult to trim and touchy to fly. Of course, in an aerobatic aeroplane this is fine, because the only long cross country flights will be en route to the competition, and we can put up with that! The rudder, however, brings a different problem, and it is necessary to thoroughly understand what is involved here.

Let us take an imaginary aeroplane, or model aeroplane, and turn it upside down. Let us also imagine that we are sitting on top of this inverted aeroplane, and that we have cut two holes in the skin so that we can reach the (inverted) rudder pedals. One further modification to our aerial curiosity is to extend the control column, through the bottom of the aeroplane, so that we, riding astride this contraption like an airborne version of Genghis Khan, can use it to fly the machine.

Inverted flight

Now if we ignore the fact that the aeroplane is really upside down, from our elevated position on the inverted belly, we can fly it quite normally, and all the controls work in the correct sense. If we bank to the left, naturally we put the stick to the left. At the same time, our original pilot, strapped firmly into his cockpit, will see his "end" of the control column move to the left. No problem here, then. Similarly if we want to climb, we pull the stick back, and our inverted pilot will see his "end" of the stick move forwards. Again all very simple.

Inverted flight: Straight and level; climbing; turning.

However, if you want to yaw to the left, naturally we push with the left foot; but inside the aeroplane, our pilot sees the right pedal move forwards! We can see that we are yawing left, but our inverted pilot will see a yaw to the right. Now we have the explanation of the apparent control reversal. It all depends upon your point of view.

If we wish to turn to the left, we apply left aileron and a touch of left rudder; then, at the desired bank angle, we hold off a little bank, and lift the nose to provide the extra lift needed by pulling very slightly back on the stick.

Let us now follow this operation from the viewpoint of our inverted pilot. The stick moves to the left together with a touch of *right* rudder; then, at the desired bank angle, we hold off a little bank, and push the stick forward slightly to provide the extra lift needed for the turn.

It becomes apparent that whether we are erect or inverted, if we want to turn left, we must apply left aileron, and vice versa. However, if we are inverted, the yaw resulting from the selected bank angle will be opposite to the direction in which we rolled, in this case it will be a yaw to the right, although to an outside observer on the ground, the aeroplane will be in a steady turn to the left. Both are correct: it all depends on the observers viewpoint. It is very important to understand this problem very clearly before progressing further.

If we now return to our Stampe, we know that straight and level flight inverted is achieved with the leading edge of the centre section in line with the horizon as seen from the rear seat: this is, of course, key point "B". If we bank to the left, we will need a touch of right rudder to balance the turn. Now our attention is drawn to a very basic instrument, the inverted slip indicator. This is a conventional slip indicator mounted upside down at the top of the panel, and it is used in exactly the same way as the normal slip indicator in erect flight, that is, we push the ball back in with the appropriate foot, e.g. ball to the right, push the right foot forward, erect or inverted, it makes no difference. Just remember to use the correct slip indicator for the attitude! As this is done, because we have no lateral stability inverted, the bank angle increases, the nose drops, and off we go into a screaming spiral dive, upside down! Many people panic, and pull back on the stick, which only worsens the situation. The solution is very simple; return to key point "B", by using the ailerons to level the wings inverted, centralise the rudder, and push gently on the

Turn and Slip Indicator —
Left Drawing: Straight and Level erect —
Right Drawing: Straight and Level inverted

stick until the nose comes up, then we can start all over again. Later we will get used to the amount of bank that we must hold off, and the pitch attitude needed to maintain height. To begin with, do not exceed 30° bank in these inverted turns, as one then has to push quite hard to keep the nose up (think of the normal steep turn), and this can be very tiring, especially if one is not used to high negative *g*.

Orientation is the biggest problem during the inverted turn, indeed, in any form of inverted flying, and one should get used to turning through 90°, then 180°, and finally 360° in both directions.

If, for example, you are inverted and wish to turn in the direction of your right wingtip, you will need right rudder, therefore left stick. Never get worried about attitude changes in inverted flight, in fact it is a good idea to move the aircraft around say, 30° in pitch and bank, always returning to key point "B" if anything goes wrong. Don't forget to roll out to erect flight frequently to rest both the engine and yourself, and don't overdo it first time out. Ten minutes thinking on the ground is worth thirty minutes floundering in the air.

Outside turn

Try to remain relaxed during inverted flying, because if you become tense you will increase the blood pressure to the upper body and head unnecessarily. If you have forgotten your early lessons in strapping in, you will be forcibly reminded here, because the continuous outside turn, is one of the most physically demanding of all manoeuvres, due to its relatively long duration. If the shoulder straps are too tight you will have difficulty in breathing·and may get light headed. If this occurs, roll out into erect flight, and brace as though you were pulling positive *g* otherwise you may "black out" for a few seconds. To protect yourself against this, tighten your lap straps and especially the negative *g* strap — this is the important one. And never, never pull through from an inverted flying exercise.

11   Acceleration

In the early days of road and rail transport, it used to be thought that man would perish if he were to exceed 30 miles per hour in one of these conveyances, although nobody could really say what he was expected to die of. Similarly people used to believe that if one fell off a tall building one was usually dead before reaching the ground. This may seem ridiculous to us in these days of space travel, but these were the beliefs of not many years ago. Nowadays we are earnestly informed that the speed of light is an impassable barrier, but barriers have an unfortunate habit of being broken.

During my early flying career I was informed by knowledgeable aeromedical lecturers that $-2g$ was about the limit that man could withstand, and we were subjected to horrifying pictures of what would happen to anyone who exceeded that figure. The fact that outside manoeuvres were banned in the RAF strengthened these arguments in everybody's mind. All the text books described the effects of excess g both positive and negative, and indeed, we all sampled the results of pulling high positive g when we reached "greyout" or even "blackout".

As a direct result of vertical acceleration, as experienced in pulling out of a dive, one naturally feels a heavy pressure against the seat, and one's limbs and head are weighed down. At first one experiences difficulty in holding one's head up, but this soon becomes semi-automatic. As the blood is drained away from the head, the first faculty to deteriorate is vision. This is manifested in the form of a loss of peripheral vision, called "tunnel' vision, because that is exactly what it looks like, and at the same time, one becomes less receptive to a light source, so that it appears that daylight is giving way to twilight. Eventually the tunnel closes, and visual blackout results, during which one can hear the engine running, and feel the controls. Effectively, one has become temporarily blinded. As the brain loses more blood, the situation becomes more confused, so that one does not usually realise that one has just lost hearing and then become unconcious;

it is only when one slowly regains conciousness and then suddenly realises with a start that one is at the controls of an aeroplane that it becomes obvious that all has not been well. It is rather like coming round in the dentist's chair; it isn't really happening, its all a bad dream. In fact many people refuse to believe they have lost conciousness when they have just been out stone cold!

The most dangerous thing about this is the period of disorientation which follows recovery from a blackout; one is not really functioning for several minutes after such an experience.

I once saw a pilot practicing for a competition after coming straight from work; he had had nothing to eat since breakfast. He had, in his sequence, a vertical 8, which involved flying an outside loop, followed immediately by a downward inside loop. The combination of no food and the rapid and fierce transition from negative to positive *g* put him out as effectively as switching off a light. The manoeuvre finished in the right place, upside down at low speed, but with no hands on the controls. The nose dropped, and the machine went into an inverted spiral dive, with apparent evil designs on the nearby village church! Fortunately this blackout only lasts as long as the *g* is applied with a healthy individual, but the disorientation could be seen from the ground as he tried to work out which way he was up, and what was going on! He learned a sharp lesson that day: never go flying on an empty stomach.

One's *g* threshold changes, not only from day to day, but also during the day. It depends upon one's general state of health, and even on whether one is contented or depressed. It lowers as one becomes tired, even during the course of one flight, but it can be controlled to a large extent by the ability of the pilot to develop his abdominal muscles to the point where he can cut off or at least reduce the flow of blood to the legs, and thus maintain a minimum pressure in the head. I personally have a threshold of nine to ten *g* for a short period, because the value of *g* must be related to the duration. If this period were increased to half a minute, I would be down to 7*g*. Almost everyone can increase

Seating position suitable for High 'G'

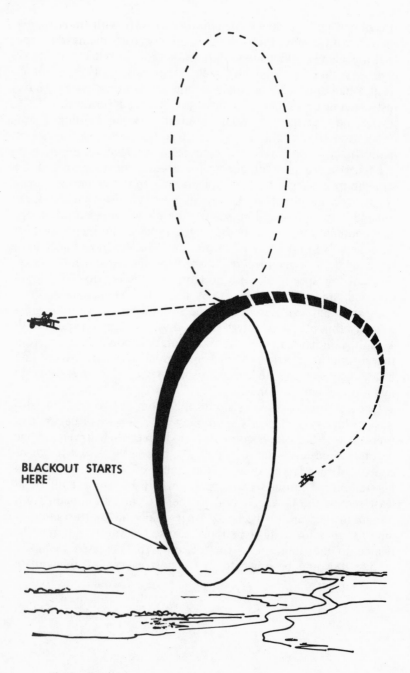

BLACKOUT STARTS
HERE

Positive 'G' tolerance reduced by preceding Negative 'G' manœuvre

their *g* tolerance by training, though to start with, most people greyout at about 5*g*. In general, short, stocky people have a better *g* tolerance than tall thin people, although there are always notable exceptions to every rule. The position of the seat in the cockpit is very important, because, if the legs are held more or less horizontal, or if one is in a semi-reclining position with the knees up, one can withstand a much higher *g* loading, as the "head pressure" of blood is reduced. All of this is rather uncomfortable, but one must learn to live with it if one intends to fly aerobatics. In time one gets used to it, but combating the effects of *g* can be extremely tiring. One usually notices it just when one's manoeuvres start to deteriorate, and very often people make the mistake of struggling on trying to correct their errors, when in fact the sensible thing to do is to land and have a rest.

A point which all aerobatic pilots ought to watch is the fact that the result of bracing against positive *g* is to compress all the warning signs into a very small area, so that the slightest relaxation will cause instant loss of conciousness. When one is braced against very high acceleration, say 9*g*, one has similar sensations to those produced by skin-diving; a singing in the ears, and a feeling of pressure change.

I was once talked into riding in the human centrifuge at Farnborough, on the pretext that it was the only way I would be able to regain clearance to fly aerobatics following an aircraft crash in which I had been concussed. As it turned out, the real reason why I was required was that I was known to be a high *g* subject, and they already had a captive low *g* subject; the idea was to compare our reactions to find out why some people were better able to withstand *g* than others. The low *g* subject was started off at $1\frac{1}{2}$ and went up by increments of $\frac{1}{2}g$, while I was subjected to 6*g* as a starter, increasing by increments of two. At 8*g*, well braced, I was fully concious and functional, and I felt the cage beginning to decelerate, whereupon I thought "that was no problem", and relaxed. Unfortunately I was still receiving the benefit of about $7\frac{1}{2}g$, and I went out like the proverbial light! When one really loses conciousness under extreme positive *g* it is very similar to an epileptic fit, and limbs and head flail uncontrollably. This happened to me, and I connected with a whole range of sharp projections in the cage, adding to the injuries I had received in the aircraft. But the worst part was the confusion and disorientation as I came round, with the cage shuddering to a stop under the action of the emergency brake. With the deceleration, as the cage swung in, I felt as though I was somer-saulting forwards. Apart from the electric light in the cage, it was dark, and the general impression I had was that I had gone off the road at night in a car, and I was now crashing into a wood! The vibration, the noise, the deceleration and the tumbling sensation all contributed to this sensation. Everything suddenly stopped, and try as I might, I could not remember where I was or what had happened, until the doctor in charge opened the door of the cage, and realization dawned. It was infinitely worse than the experience of actually crashing in an aeroplane, and was a dramatic demonstration of the result of relaxing under high *g*. The less one tenses, the softer and more widely spaced are the symptoms. Nowadays I tense, but I don't relax until the *g* is definitely off! And not for anything will I ever go near the centrifuge again!.

Quite a lot is known about positive *g* these days and also zero *g*, especially after all the space research, but surprisingly little is known of that more sinister acceleration negative *g*.

Our early aeromedical lecturers used to go into alarming detail in the description of a phenomenon called redout, which was the result of an outside loop, where the blood, instead of draining away from the head, was slammed back under cruel and alarming pressure. A negative *g* value of -2 was as much as one could be expected to stand; $-4g$ was considered lethal, as it would undoubtedly cause a brain haemorrhage.

My first encounter with this sort of acceleration also resulted in a "redout", a phenomenon which has not occurred since, in spite of much higher negative loadings. I now believe that it was caused by the lower eyelid being pulled up over the eye by gravity, and one could then look through the taut membrane as one can do if one places a hand over an electric torch.

I have gradually increased the loading over the years, and with each increment the medics have said "well, maybe, but one more *g* would be dangerous". In the end some of them believe that one can accept as much negative *g* as positive, but the real answer is that they don't know.

It is certain that negative *g* is dangerous. One can become acclimatised to a certain extent, and careful strapping in with a good negative *g* strap can certainly alleviate it. Also if one is able to relax, the effects are minimised. It is extremely tiring in the early stages, although I now prefer it to positive *g*; at least I don't have to brace, and the tendency to blackout is less. Yes, blackout, in spite of the increased blood pressure; this too can cause tunnel vision; the only difference that the edges of the tunnel are sharp and clear, not blurred as in positive g loadings. Negative g can also cause temporary deafness, so that one cannot even hear the engine! But beware! Take it slowly, and watch for the warning signs. When I'm overdoing it I get pins and needles in the scalp, and if this happens I ease off instantly. The next stage is literally "seeing stars", and this I believe to be the fringe of a really hazardous condition. You can expect bruising from the safety harness, and bloodshot eyes where the small vessels have ruptured, There is also a sensation of grit behind the eyeballs when this happens. Under negative g one can feel the eyeballs swelling up with blood; it is not comfortable, but feels worse than it is. Sometimes one feels that the head is under great pressure, and headaches can be a result of overdoing things. Gradually the vessels in the eyes are able to cope with the pressure, so that these days red eyes are a thing of the past, in spite of pushing up to −6g. However, you will find that you can no longer tolerate smoky atmospheres or late nights due to the extreme eye irritation. Fresh air and plenty of sleep are the best remedies.

One can go from +9g to −5g with no problem of loss of vision or conciousness; the sensation is as though somebody has opened the doors of a blast furnace, such is the dramatic temperature increase as the blood rushes savagely into the head. One never gets cold in winter, even in an open cockpit, when flying aerobatics, for this reason, and because of the physical work involved in maoeuvring the aeroplane .

We have already seen that while positive to negative is no problem, going from as little as −1 to +4 can cause blackout, so one must brace hard as the pull comes on. However, do not make the mistake of bracing whilst still under negative g; the result can be a sudden and splitting headache which can jeopardise the control of the aircraft.

It is as well to keep the sortie length to twenty minutes as the tiring effects of negative g can be very insidious, and can cause errors in thinking as well as flying.

A colleague of mine was once subjected to a steady −3g on the infamous centrifuge, for which purpose he had been connected to a device to monitor his heartbeat. During the run, he subsequently told us, he had felt "rather queer", and the emergency brake had been used to stop the centrifuge. When he later saw the traces, the reasons for the emergency stop became perfectly clear; his heart had stopped!

The moral is obvious; if you don't feel well, at any time, not only should you stop the aerobatic sequence, you should land as as soon as possible. Don't take any chances; we don't know a great deal about negative *g*.

12 *Limitations*

Having seen the limitations of the human frame under stress, it is as well to consider what is happening to the aeroplane during all this. To appreciate this properly it is necessary to understand a little about the design philosophy of an aerobatic aeroplane, and to have a basic grasp of some of the aerodynamics involved.

One might consider that the frail human body would fail long before a machine which is designed to fly aerobatics, so why worry? The answer is that under certain conditions, the human body can survive undamaged through a situation that will destroy the aeroplane: it is partly a product of speed and acceleration, and partly the duration of the manoeuvre which produces this situation. A good example is to consider the cartridge operated ejection seat, which subjects the pilot to about 25*g*! I have yet to see the aeroplane that could withstand that sort of acceleration!

To satisfy the civil airworthiness requirements the aerobatic aeroplane must conform to factors, which have as their basis strength and stiffness. The strength is measured by the forces which can be applied to the machine without breaking it, while the stiffness is related to the tendency towards flutter, control reversal, and divergence. When an aerobatic aeroplane is designed, the maximum acceleration to which it will be subjected is decided upon, both positive and negative. This is called the limit load, and is the figure to which we should operate during aerobatics; it is indicated by red painted lines on the accelerometer. Of course the manufacturer has to prove that his machine will accept these loads, and he will subject the aircraft to a static load which usually, but not always, exceeds the limit load by up to 133%; and this is called the proof loading. Sometimes the proof load is the same as the limit load, but although the structure may distort under proof load, it must always return to its original state when the load is removed. As an added safety feature, the aircraft is required to withstand a load one and a half times greater than the limit load, without collapse, although there will almost certainly be structural damage, and this is called the ultimate load. It should be noted that these figures are required for British certification purposes, so that certain foreign amateur built aircraft may have a lower factor of safety.

6'G'

Also, a glance at a typical V—n diagram will show that the limit load may only be utilised in the middle speed band, usually between the manoeuvre speed (Va) and the cruising speed (Vc). It will be seen that there is a linear cutoff above cruising speed up to VD (design diving speed) and at this speed the permitted levels of g may be very low indeed. The ability to pull excessive g below Va is usually limited by the curved line representing the stall.

In all these cases, the factors are quoted for symmetric flight, i.e. no rolling or yawing, and if these parameters are present, because of the twisting effect on the structure, the maximum permitted g (limit load) is a good deal lower.

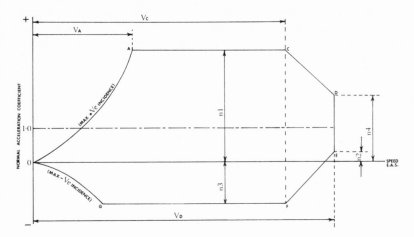

Typical V-a Diagram

All this boils down to the fact that we cannot pull up to the red line on the accelerometer at every point in the speed range without exceeding the limit load. Also we will have to be careful during rolling pullouts to restrict the *g* applied; on many aircraft Pilots Notes quote maximum *g* values for half aileron and full aileron rolling pullouts.

In particular the *g* achieved in the flickroll can exceed the permitted figure by a good margin, and this is why there are relatively low limits in terms of airspeed for executing this manoeuvre. There have been many instances of damage involving twisting of the fuselage due to flickrolling at too high a speed.

It is quite easy to overstress an aerobatic aeroplane, even if one is being careful; for example, during the pullout from a manoeuvre, if one is pulling hard and then hits the slipstream, the accelerometer will tell the tale. All we will have felt in the cockpit is a slight jolt, which will not concern us physically in the least, but the structure may have suffered. Although there may be no evidence of damage, any overstress should be reported on landing; it may hurt your pride, but it is better than seeing a friend involved in a structural failure. Each time the machine is overstressed, its fatigue life is reduced: as an example, the Zlin 526A is certificated for $+6$ and $-3g$, and its aerobatic life under these conditions is 2200 hours. If this machine is flown to competition standards, as has been done by two European countries, using $+8$ and $-6g$, the airframe life is reduced to 100 hours. Fatigue in metal is cumulative, and there is no real way of measuring it; when it reaches its critical point, it fails without warning, although if careful inspection procedures are used, it may be possible to detect the beginning of a crack.'

I have been in the unenviable situation of having a wing collapse in an aerobatic aeroplane due to fatigue, brought on by many accidental overstresses over a long period. Since the wing folded upwards, I very soon lost control of the aircraft, and it wasn't until I managed to get it upside down that the wing came back into position with an almighty bang. Having no parachute, I was faced with the problem of how to land an aeroplane that would only fly inverted without the wing folding. The fact that I am here at all is due to my having a detailed knowledge of the structure of that particular aeroplane, plus a very large slice of that abstract parameter we call luck! You should make it your business to understand very clearly the construction and operation of your aeroplane; your life may depend upon it.

ZLIN Accelerometer after typical training sortie

So far we have considered vertical acceleration; but of course there are other limitations too, and here we may consider the implications of structural stiffness. This is designed into an aeroplane with the intention that the aircraft shall not significantly twist, bend, or otherwise distort, inside the speed envelope. The situation outside this envelope is another matter! I have seen pilots trying to achieve a manoeuvre by the simple expedient of entering it faster and faster, obviously working on the assumption that if you move it fast enough, even a brick will eventually fly! Aerobatic aeroplanes are no different to ordinary machines in that they are made of the same materials and governed by the same laws of aerodynamics. All aeroplanes are so designed that they are not dangerously sensitive to distortion at any speed up to at least 1·2 VD. Now VNE is the maximum figure we are allowed to reach, much less VD, so one would think we were quite safe. Normally this is so, but this safety factor is influenced by vertical acceleration, and can also be degraded by backlash and wear in the control circuits, to say nothing of loose rigging in a biplane.

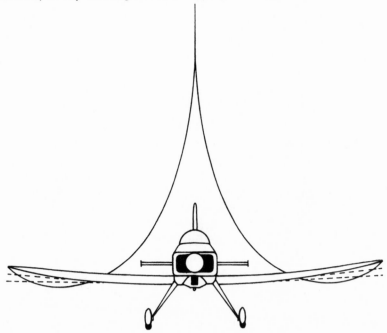

Airframe distortion at High 'G'

Before we blithely exceed VNE, let us consider not only the magnitude of the forces on the aeroplane, but also the vibration mode of the machine. No doubt we have all felt aileron "buzz" and general vibration, but this is nothing compared with wing or aileron flutter. Years ago, between the wars, many machines were lost due to this, and the onset is so rapid and fierce, that structural failure usually follows before there is any chance of recovery. Control hinge wear reduces the normal safety factor, and can bring about a situation where flutter may be encountered. Flutter is an oscillary vibration, which relies for its period on the vibratory mode of the structure, but whose amplitude is a result of airspeed. Flutter which starts on the ailerons, for example, can instantly start the whole wing going. It is sometimes possible to stop it, if one is quick, by putting a very small sideclip on the aeroplane, or to use aileron trim and hold the force on the stick, whilst at the same time reducing speed, but it is very dangerous, and usually causes damage before it can be stopped. The real answer is simple – don't exceed VNE.

An aircraft may also be restricted in terms of full control application, and this defines the manoeuvre speed (Va), which is derived from both the strength and stiffness requirements of the controls and the basic structure. It is the maximum speed at which the pilot may fully deflect the controls.

Having covered the airframe in some detail, it is worth looking at the power plant. The most obvious factor is the possibility of exceeding the maximum rpm, and this can result in not only con-rod stretch, valve bounce, and so on, but will also reduce engine life. Another result of over-revving is that the temperature within the engine will increase, and perhaps not evenly, so that there is a real danger of straightforward failure brought on by temperature extremes, and also failures due to the breakdown in the lubricating properties of the oil at high temperature. During aerobatic flying, the oil pressure should be carefully monitored – engines don't like running without oil!

There are vibration ranges in most engines which will produce a fatigue situation, and the same applies to propellers; these rpm bands are unlikely to coincide, so one has to be careful to avoid them as much as possible. Propeller vibration is very serious and there may be two or three vibration ranges within the permitted engine range. This, coupled with the high gyroscopic forces resulting from flick rolls, power on spins, etc., can cause failures of the propeller blades or crankshaft.

These same forces can cause engine bearer failures, so particular attention should be paid to this area on the preflight inspection; it is very difficult to control an aircraft once the engine has parted company.

While you may have been staying within the limits, it doesn't necessarily follow that everyone else has; so it is a wise move to assume that they have not. The accelerometer should have been left by the previous pilot for you to see, and he should have reported any defects or suspicions he may have had. Even if you do a "running change" (changing pilots without stopping the engine), have a general look at the shape of the aircraft, and watch out for tell tale signs such as wrinkled skin or fabric. If in doubt, shut down and investigate. Even very small things could point to something much more serious. Just recently I noticed that the canopy on an aerobatic aircraft appeared to be rattling more than usual, although everything else seemed satisfactory. On closer inspection a small area of wrinkled fabric was noticed on the side of the fuselage below the windscreen. This was eventually opened up, to reveal a fractured longeron!

The manufacturers investigated this and stated that in their opinion the failure had been caused by flick rolling at excessive speed. This time we were lucky and had picked it up before there was a major accident.

But it just goes to show that you can't be too careful. Observe the limitations, report any mistakes which have resulted in exceeding them, and pay attention to little things which may be trying to give you warning. Take your time on the external inspection: better twenty minutes late in this world than twenty years early in the next!

13   *Developing the roll*

Flick roll

Armed with information on the limitations of the aeroplane, we are now able to combine the three planes of freedom into one manoeuvre to give us the flick roll. This is an autorotational figure over which we have a certain degree of control, although, having initiated it, normally it will continue of its own accord until either we elect to stop it, or it falls into a spin. It is really, in its basic form, one turn of a spin in horizontal flight, entered from a "high speed", or dynamic, stall.

Since the drag will be very high, the speed decay in the figure will be quite dramatic, so that in order to be able to recover effectively, one must enter at as high a speed as possible, within the limitations.

This results in one given entry speed which is approximately twice the power off stalling speed: however pilots' notes should be consulted for each type of aeroplane, as the speed in some cases may be lower. Flick rolls are not normally entered at much below the declared speed because there is then a good chance that the aircraft will overshoot and go into a spin, even with full recovery control applied, due simply to the very low speed in the recovery which prevents the controls from being sufficiently effective. Aircraft with high wing loadings flick much better than low wing loading types, and are easier to stop precisely. One has only to compare the Jungmeister with the Stampe, or the Pitts Special with the Tiger Moth. The flick roll is usually much faster "with" the engine, and has a clearer entry, but is more difficult to stop: on the other hand, if stopping it is a problem, it is often better to go "against" the engine, which results in a slower rotation, but more control at the end. The engine can also be used to speed up or slow down the flick.

The primary controls used in the flick roll are the elevator and rudder; the ailerons, although used in some cases, are generally held neutral throughout. With some aircraft, they are used conventionally, to assist the roll, while with others, they are used opposite to the rudder to help to stall the downgoing wing.

We will, however, consider the flick roll without the use of ailerons. In the Stampe the maximum practical speed for entry is 70 knots. Since one is often accelerating into a flick roll, any delay will inevitably result in a higher speed during entry, and we may recall that the absolute maximum speed for a Stampe is twice the stalling speed, i.e. 76 knots: this is why we try and aim for 70 knots to begin with. The type of propeller fitted will materially alter the characteristics in the flick: I once flew a Stampe with a metal propeller which would scarcely flick at all! With the standard wooden propeller the Stampe will flick roll marginally better to the right, but the technique is basically the same for both directions. Reduce speed to about 50 knots, and apply full power, maintaining level flight. As the speed reaches 68 knots, lift the nose fractionally, and then apply full rudder and a split second after initiating this, pull the stick smoothly and smartly fully back. It is important to realise that the rudder and stick movements are not separate; they occur almost simultaneously, with the rudder slightly leading the stick. The sensation is very like a high speed spin, which, of course, it is. The rotation is very rapid, and exact timing is important. However, it is unlikely that a good recovery will be achieved first time, though this does not matter, as the worst that can happen is a normal spin.

As the aircraft reaches the inverted position the stick is returned to a point just aft of neutral; now that the rotation is well under way we do not need the high angle of attack required to initiate: indeed, this would be an embarrassment, as the drag would be very high. With the lower angle of attack, we are still stalled, and the roll continues undiminished. As we enter the last quarter of the roll, we must initiate recovery. The exact number of degrees before the wings level position where this must be done will depend on

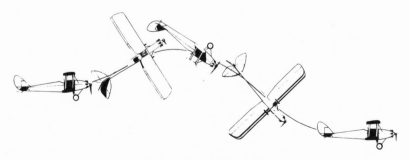

Positive Flick Roll – right

the airspeed, angle of attack achieved, and rate of control application. Recovery is the same as for the spin, but much more rapid; i.e. full rudder to oppose the yaw, and stick forward, fully forward if necessary. When the roll has stopped, use all three controls normally to keep straight and to maintain height, and it is here that we will need full power to accelerate the aircraft away from the fringe of the stall, as one can easily lose 30 knots in a flick roll.

Although full power is normally used, it may help in the early stages to reduce power to recover from a flick roll to the right, since full left rudder used "against" the engine may not stop the rotation. Similarly, half power may be used to initiate a faster flick roll to the left, "against" the engine, and in this case, full power will not only help to stop the roll, but will also give good acceleration.

In certain very high performance aeroplanes, such as the Pitts Special, one may wish to go "against" the engine in order to slow down the fantastic rotational speed of the flick roll.

The biggest problem in the early stages is the control of the speed during entry, and a look at the accelerometer ought to convince anybody that 76 knots really is the limit! Admittedly the higher speeds give a cleaner manoeuvre, but remember that the aircraft will not fly without its wings! With all flicks, the timing is critical, and there is no need to be vicious with the controls. The secret of all flick rolling is to reduce the angle of attack slightly after the flick starts, to retain as much airspeed as possible.

Another way of flick rolling, which will allow you to complete the manoeuvre more easily is to pull up from 75 knots, and with the nose about 15° above the horizon, with the stick coming back steadily all the time, just give the rudder a gentle tap: the aeroplane will rotate quickly and smoothly, with no shuddering or buffeting.

Flick Roll going wrong at low altitude

This is not a competition figure, but it is easy on the aeroplane. Should you encounter buffeting at any time, you may be sure you have pulled the stick back too soon and too hard.

A word of caution about flick rolling low wing loading aeroplanes like the Stampe; don't do it too low. No matter how many times it worked perfectly at 3,000 feet, you can be sure that if you do it at 300 feet it will go wrong! Some years ago I reached the finals of the Lockheed Aerobatic Trophy in a Stampe, and my final manoeuvre was a variation on the flick roll. It worked every time, at 300 feet, including during the contest. Next day, for no particular reason, I did it again, at 1,000 feet, this time. It did another turn, and I finished upside down, stalled, out of control. I regained level flight at 500 feet!

Of all aerobatic manoeuvres, the flick roll is the one most likely to let you down at the worst possible moment, so keep them up high enough to give you chance to recover if the worst happens.

Hesitation rolls

These are all a variation of the basic slow roll, and we may expect to encounter 3, 4, 6 and 8 point rolls in competition, although 12 pointers used to be common and the 16 and 32 point rolls make an interesting exercise, however the latter could be confused with a slightly shaky slow roll. The technique is precisely the same as with the slow roll, except that one pauses every 90° in the case of the 4 point roll, 45° in the case of the 8 pointer, and so on. Because of these pauses, the overall roll takes longer to complete, therefore more speed is needed.

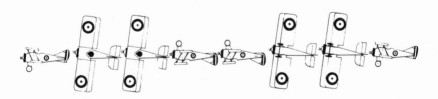

Hesitation Roll

In the Stampe 105 to 110 knots is quite sufficient, although a good 4 point roll can be done at 85 knots. When the aircraft is held at the 90° point with the wings vertical, all the lift must come from the side of the fuselage, and if the nose is up, the inclined thrust vector from the engine.

Although some aeroplanes will fly on their side, the Stampe will not, and so one must lift the nose high enough to start with to allow for it to drop a little at this point. Also aileron drag causes sudden and unwanted turning moments, especially as one approaches the inverted, requiring considerable applications of opposite rudder, the result of which is to slow down the roll. This slowing down occurs at point 2 of a 4 point roll, and between points 3 and 4 of an 8 point roll) therefore the roll rate here must be anticipated and the earlier points slowed down to match it. Also, due to the normal roll-with-sideslip effects at points 7 and 8 of an 8 point roll, the roll tends to speed up. It is a good idea to count aloud to oneself, trying to keep time like a metronome, and to deliberately try to slow down the last points. In all of this, key point "B" must still be achieved at the midway point of the roll. At the three-quarter point in the roll the nose is really trying to drop, so if one cannot keep it up without extreme use of rudder, let it drop and as soon as the wings level, raise the nose to the level flight attitude.

This correction will be noticed less than using a bootful of rudder. The best looking figure is achieved when the roll rate matches the timing of the hesitations. All these rolls may be started from inverted flight; the principle is exactly the same except that one flies the second half of the roll before the first half.

Barrel roll

Not often seen in competition these days, the barrel roll is nevertheless a good co-ordination manoeuvre, and is not properly understood by a great many pilots. It is a very gentle manoeuvre, and requires a high level of skill to fly it well. One may look upon it as a cross between a loop and a roll, in that with a machine that rolls slowly, like the Tiger Moth, the nose has to be so high to enable the machine to get round, that it looks almost like a twisted loop.

The aim is to describe a helix in the sky, the corkscrew path of the aeroplane tracing the outline of a barrel; hence the name.

In the Air Force we were taught to turn the nose away from our axis so that we could then draw a circle in the sky with the nose of the aeroplane, using the axis as a centre point. In competition flying, we start and finish aligned with the axis and have a displaced centre spot for the roll.

This central spot must be visualised as being above the horizon, which will result in the aircraft being banked vertically when the nose is above the spot, but more important, it will allow the wings to reach the level position inverted before the nose falls through the horizon. This is to prevent great loss of height during the last part of the roll.

Again, at the three-quarter mark, the wings are vertically banked as the nose passes below the centre spot, and the roll continues until the wings are once again level. In contrast to all the other rolls, the slipball stays in the middle all the way round, and there is no negative *g* involved.

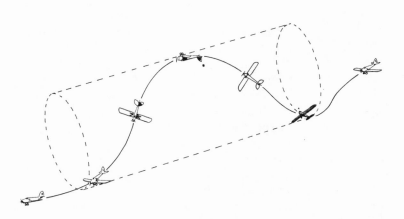

Barrel Roll

A very common fault with the barrel roll is to roll too slowly to start with, so that the nose comes down through the horizon before the wings are level inverted. The result of this is a high speed spiral dive, with considerable height loss.

The barrel roll is a very good manoeuvre to fly in almost any aerobatic or semi-aerobatic aeroplane, and is a good figure to demonstrate to a passenger who doesn't want to suffer too much *g*. An old friend of mine used to barrel roll his monoplane with his pet greyhound sitting placidly on the back seat! He also once did it with a pint of beer on board, without spilling any!

Rolling circles

Up to now we have covered basic figures which most pilots have known for half a century. With the rolling circle we are beginning to come up to date as we attempt a manoeuvre which is intricate and demanding, requiring a high level of co-ordination to fly, but resulting in one of the most flowing, graceful figures to be seen.

There are many different kinds of rolling circle, in fact there is no limit to the number of rolls which one can insert in a 360° turn, and of course the value of the turn is not limited to 360°. For the moment, we shall ignore fractions and multiples of turns, and consider the manoeuvre within the framework of a 360° horizontal circle. Commonly, in present day competitions, one may have one, two, three or four rolls in such a circle. The circle may start and finish erect or inverted, and the rolls may be in the same direction as the turn, or against it, or a combination of both. One may even have different types of roll in one circle, e.g. slow, 4 point, 8 point, barrel, and so on. We shall confine ourselves here to the basic 4-roll circle, whilst appreciating that we are merely scratching the surface; but the principles discussed here will hold good for all the others.

The intention is to fly a 4-roll circle, rolling inwards, that is, in the same direction as the turn, starting and finishing erect. Since the drag is high, the speed will quickly stabilise at a figure between the climbing speed and the cruising speed, depending on the power available, so there is no need to dive to gain speed. Full power is used throughout, and again key point "B" is very important; we shall achieve it four times in this figure. The direction of roll and turn are not important, except with respect to each other, and as with all handed figures they should be practised both to left and right.

From the study of the figure it becomes clear that we must fly 4° of roll for every degree of turn, or, we may wish to look at it in the sense that for every roll, we must turn 90°. The use of a model is very helpful in understanding exactly what is required.

We can further break the figure down by considering only a quarter of the circle with one roll, as the remainder of the figure is then merely a repetition.

We start, therefore, in level flight at full power, and we are going to roll and turn left, in this case. We look out to the left and pick two points on the horizon, one at 45° to the left of the nose, and one at 90°, on the wingtip. Left aileron is then smoothly and steadily applied, as is left rudder, to start the nose skidding left;

this is going to feel the most unco-ordinated manoeuvre in the world, but it relies on the 4:1 roll/turn relationship for absolute perfection. As the bank increases towards the vertical, the turn is assisted with elevator, still holding a steady roll rate, and the rudder is now coming on to the right much later than in the slow roll. At the same time, the forward stick pressure is delayed because otherwise it would slow down the rate of turn. Now, as the wings reach the inverted position we are using almost full right rudder to skid the nose hard around the horizon, and we are able to check at the same time that we have achieved key point "B" and the 45° mark. Once again the wings approach the vertical and now we are pushing hard forward on the stick in our efforts to keep the turn going, while at the same time the rudder is again reversing through neutral. With the wings approaching level again, hard left rudder is being used to skid the nose round to the 90° point. We are really using all the control available, and the visual effect is that the engine cowling is a ball which we are rolling around the rim of the horizon. Without a pause in the roll rate we snatch a glance to the left to pick up new 45° and 90° marks, and repeat the sequence, four times in all for the complete manoeuvre. At the same time we must ensure that the nose is not rising and falling like a switchback, which it tends to do at first, and finally the circle must be exactly round.

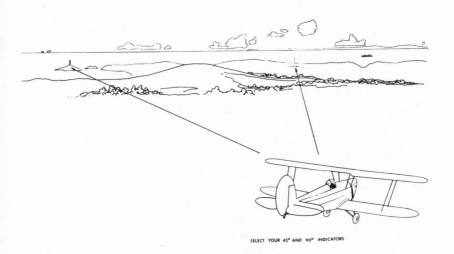

SELECT YOUR 45° AND 90° INDICATORS

Commencement of rolling circle

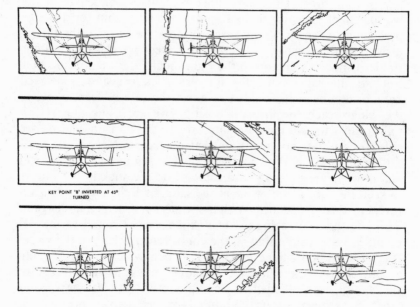

Rolling Circle (inwards) first quarter

If we have to adjust the shape of the circle in the air due to wind, so that we fly the perfect shape over the ground, we must also adjust the roll and turn rate to suit. No wonder it is a high pointed figure!

To roll "against" the turn, i.e. to fly an "outward" rolling circle, the same general principles apply: only the initial start is slightly difficult because one has to push the stick forward as the manoeuvre starts, and this usually results in the aeroplane descending not fully under control initially.

Let us once again assume a left turn, but this time with a right roll. The manoeuvre is best started by lifting the nose a shade, and then starting what is almost a slow roll to the right. At the same time, considerable left rudder is used to skid the nose to the left, and the forward stick is brought in early, and positively, also to help the turn. As the wings approach level with the nose swinging up a shade higher than key point "B", we note that the 45° mark is on the nose. The rudder, meantime has now reversed and is skidding the nose to our "right" as we sit inverted. The rudder stays on to keep the nose up as the wings reach vertical and we can now pull back on the stick to assist the turn. Approaching level flight once again we initially release only enough right rudder to allow the nose to turn 1° for every 4° we roll, and as we pass the 90° point the rudder is smoothly reversed to help swing the nose left and up into the next quarter. Now that it is under way, the "outward" rolling circle is easier than the "inverted". Three, **two**, and one roll circles can be flown using the same techniques, but with fewer rolls in a circle one approaches the limit of available control. The difficulty is always to try and keep the turn going steadily when the wings are level, and this is where strong inherent directional stability is a big disadvantage. If the machine will fly reasonably well on its side the figure will be easier; also the bigger the circle, within reasonable limits, the slower the roll rate, and the easier it gets.

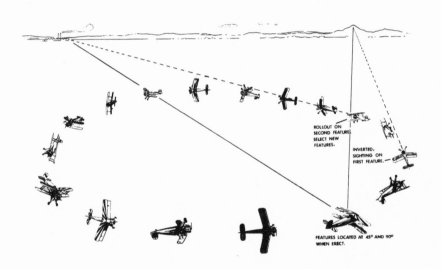

ROLLOUT ON SECOND FEATURE. SELECT NEW FEATURES.

INVERTED, SIGHTING ON FIRST FEATURE.

FEATURES LOCATED AT 45° AND 90° WHEN ERECT.

Rolling Circle (outwards)

Starting a rolling circle from the inverted position always seems to cause problems, but with our model we can see that once we have started rolling, it is exactly the same as if we had started from erect flight. The only problems are orientating oneself on an axis which is 45° from the old axis when we are erect, and knowing which way to start rolling and applying elevator. I personally never use any axis for reference except the main axis used for the sequence as a whole, and I look at it rather than at the horizon, but that is

One turn Rolling Circle (outward)

something we have to decide for ourselves. It is also a good idea
to count off either the rolls or the degrees turned through, as it is
quite easy to get lost!

14 Developing the loop

Avalanche

We have seen that most aerobatic manoeuvres are a result of combination figures, and the most common example which we come across where two complete figures are combined is in the avalanche. Strangely enough, this manoeuvre does not appear in the Aresti dictionary, although one has the basic information to construct it. Known also as the Porteous Loop, it consists of a normal inside loop with a full inside flick roll at the top. Although the aeroplane is inverted at the beginning and end of the flick roll, as we can show with the model, the flick roll is made under positive *g*, and is therefore an inside flick. Now we know from our study of the flick roll that if we enter too slowly it will wallow and

Avalanche

spin, but at the same time we must not enter it too fast. We will find that between 110 and 120 knots is a good entry speed to use, permitting a neat flick without excess speed. In any case we do not wish to waste height by diving to gain an unnecessarily high airspeed. This figure is best flown into wind, as it is even more critical than the basic loop for shape, and it will need all possible assistance from the wind. In the early stages one can become disorientated in the flick, with the result that one loses direction during the exit, so it is best flown above a good feature line to start with.

The entry to the figure is very similar, as far as the initial pitch rate is concerned, to the roll-off-the-top, but as the aircraft approaches the inverted position the pull is eased off slightly. With the nose about 15° to 20° above the horizon a normal flick roll is initiated, as if we were in level flight, except that we do not release the back pressure half way round the roll. If we were to do this the roll will either stop or it will slow down and perhaps fall off sideways. With the stick still well back the autorotation is maintained, and as the wings approach level again with the aircraft inverted, full opposite rudder is applied and almost full forward stick. At the instant the roll stops, the shape of the loop must be immediately picked up and maintained. If one recommences the loop too quickly it will be less than round, and if one delays too long, there will be an unsightly bulge in the second half. The loop should be rounded off carefully, with the exit height and speed in theory being the same as during the entry, however, because of the high drag in the flick, this cannot be, and it is best to sacrifice speed by pulling tight in the last quarter, rather than lose height and destroy the shape of the manoeuvre. One must be particularly careful not to re-stall the aeroplane in the attempt to shape the second half of the loop. It is not a good manoeuvre to fly at low altitude for these reasons; but it can be accomplished by entering at a higher speed, and pulling more gently, so that the first half of the loop is bigger: the flick can then be entered at the original speed, and a normal recovery can be made, since now there is more height available to finish the figure.

It is difficult to judge exactly where to flick in the beginning, and this only comes with practice. The biggest fault lies in flicking early or late, and where the greatest danger lies is in flicking early, perhaps near the vertical, where the speed is still very high. The obvious result will be a vertical flick roll, quite possibly followed by a tailslide with the controls still deflected, while we are still trying to sort out where the ground has gone.

The most common errors, however, are smaller than this, but we will find that regardless of whether the nose is too steep or too shallow with respect to the horizon when the flick is initiated, the exit will always be very steep, in fact, sometimes vertical. There is a very narrow band, around 15° to 20° for the Stampe, where the flick must be started. All aircraft exhibit this characteristic of finishing nose down if the start angle is wrong, although the actual starting angle for the flick will vary widely, depending upon your particular aircraft.

With the Zlin, for example, the flick starts about 5° only above the horizon, and finishes 5° down. If one can achieve equal entry and exit angles, one can be fairly sure that the flick was centrally placed in the top of the loop, which is the object of the exercise. In the case of the avalanche, most aircraft should be flicked "with" the engine, as we need all the rotational speed we can get, and the recovery is less of a problem, since the nose is down, and the aircraft is beginning to accelerate.

Square loop

This has been a little used, though much abused figure, in that there is a great tendency to place excessive strain on the aeroplane during its execution. The requirement is very simple, i.e. to trace an exactly square shape in the sky. The pitching capability is used

Square Loop

to the maximum, especially on the two bottom corners, but if one encounters stall buffet, particularly on the first corner, then the pitch rate is too great. Part of the reason why it is not seen very often is that it requires only a small error in technique to spoil the shape of the figure, and also it is easy to make a mistake and cause an overstress. Several years ago, a pilot on the Continent, who specialised in this manoeuvre, eventually used so much g on the entry that both wings came off the aeroplane! It ought to be added, though, that it was estimated that he pulled about 14g!

The square loop is entered at about 110 knots in the Stampe, and one must trace a horizontal path for a second or so before commencing, to establish the datum line of the figure. Full power is used, and the aircraft is pulled quickly into the vertical, aiming to record $5\frac{1}{2}g$ on the accelerometer (this is to allow for mistakes). As in so many other manoeuvres, it is extremely important to be able to arrest the pitching movement cleanly in the vertical, otherwise the figure will look ragged. The vertical line is held as long as possible, and the aircraft is rotated quickly in pitch and held in the inverted position; this requiring an extreme nose up attitude because of the very low airspeed. There will probably be a tendency to stall under positive g on the corner, unless real finesse is used, and during the initial part of the top of the square, the aircraft will be partially stalled inverted, which will result in buffet and aileron snatching. Here one needs a firm grip and sensitive reactions. If the aircraft tends to sink, one knows that the climbing leg was held too long, or perhaps the nose was too high on the inverted leg. There is usually no problem in getting the top corners square. Bearing in mind the extremely low speed, the time spent on the top leg will of course be longer than on the other three, and this will be further modified by the strength of the wind.

At the right moment the aircraft is pulled quickly into the vertical dive, and the throttle is normally closed at this point. This third leg also causes complication because with the ground rapidly approaching, the tendency is to cut it short, whereas it should be the same length as the climbing leg. The last corner is again flown to $5\frac{1}{2}g$ on the accelerometer, and full power is again applied, to tighten the radius, and also to maintain speed for the next figure, which should not be commenced until one has passed the original pull up point for the manoeuvre we have just flown.

The square loop is usually flown into the prevailing wind, because otherwise the time spent on the top leg makes the figure appear protracted when it is really geometrically correct. Also it allows the bottom corners to appear sharper than they really are.

The only way to establish whether the loop is really square, is for somebody to observe it from the ground, and to note the errors. A big mistake is that there is a tendency to pull harder and harder in an attempt to make the bottom corners really square, the result being an inevitable overstress. If we use our heads however, this need not happen. The question as to whether the loop is square or otherwise depends upon the relationship between the radius of the corners, and the length of the legs. We cannot tighten the corners any more without breaking something, so let us increase the length of the legs; and we do this by using a higher entry speed. Always remember, though, that at this new speed, we cannot pull as hard as we did before if we wish to keep inside the g limit. Although the radius will be larger, the length of the leg will be increased much more, by comparison, and we will have a bigger, but more pleasing, figure.

The square loop requires an aeroplane which can pitch very quickly, and this is why it is more suitable for a biplane than a monoplane. For best effect it should be flown at a relatively low altitude (during competition) because it obviously will look best exactly from the side. To achieve a good manoeuvre, the monoplane will have to fly a much bigger loop than is necessary for a biplane.

The figure can also be flown downwards from inverted flight, and in this case we can commence with the wind behind us, which will result in the same manoeuvre as above; and we can also fly just half of either of these figures, which will give us a turn-round manoeuvre.

The Octagonal loop

A development of the square loop, this figure is also called the eight sided, or eight point, loop. The same principles apply, but since one only has to pitch 45° instead of 90°, it follows that either the manoeuvre is easier on the aeroplane, or, for the same loading, much sharper angles are possible. It is far more popular than the square loop, and is seen very often in competition sequences. Here, too, there is a tendency for the last four points to be a little rushed, perhaps because it is usual for this figure to be flown at the bottom height limit, for best visual effect. With more points and lines in the figure, there is more room for error, since all angles must be equal, as must be the length of all sides, and since the speed is changing, the time interval also changes for each leg.

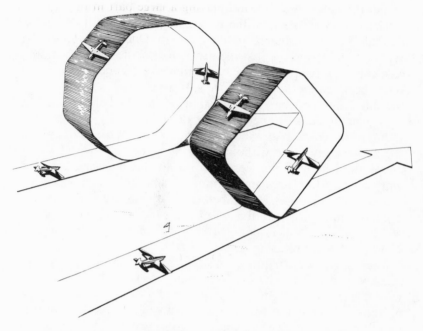

Octagonal and Diamond Loops

Because of the potential for very sharp corners, many pilots try too hard, with the result that in attempting to arrest the pitch at each point, the result is a "kickback", which is due to moving the stick so quickly that one cannot stop it from overshooting, especially if the control inertia is heavy. This looks worse than having the corners less sharp, but can be corrected either by pitching and correcting less abruptly, or by using two hands to damp the stick movement. This figure too, can be flown downwards starting inverted, and half loops, though less common, can be done.

A common error is for all points to be early or late, this resulting in a figure which is slightly inclined, forwards or backwards. Again, this can only be corrected by ground observation. All machines can fly this figure well, which perhaps accounts for its popularity.

Variations
There are endless geometric possibilities, as one can imagine, but those which are seen in competition work are restricted to triangular and hexagonal, or six-sided loops. Again the principles

remain the same, with the wind playing a large part in the shape of the figure. A variation of the square loop is to turn it through 45°, when it then becomes a diamond loop. One can also fly all these loops with various rolls incorporated in the different legs, which can result in an intricate and impressive manoeuvre.

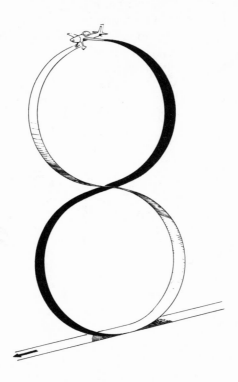

Vertical Eight

Rolling loops
This is a variation of the rolling turn; except that it is flown in the vertical plane. It is extremely difficult to fly accurately, and as such is not much in favour in present day competitions, although it makes an excellent training exercise. It really requires an aeroplane which will loop sideways, but a passable manoeuvre can be achieved with the Stampe.

Normally one sees loops with one, two, three or four rolls; and with the Stampe, which does not have a high roll rate, it is easier to fly only one roll. This means one degree of roll for every degree of pitch, because, in the contest, any variation in roll or pitch rate will lose marks. The use of a model is very helpful to see what is required, but one has four datum points; vertically up, with 90° of roll; level on top, right way up; vertically down, with 270° of roll; and level, erect, at the bottom, theoretically at the same height and speed as the start, but in practice it is hard to maintain height.

If one looks at this figure end on, one sees a very drunken track weaved through the sky, since there has to be an element of push and pull in order to best utilise wing lift; but hopefully this is not seen from the side.

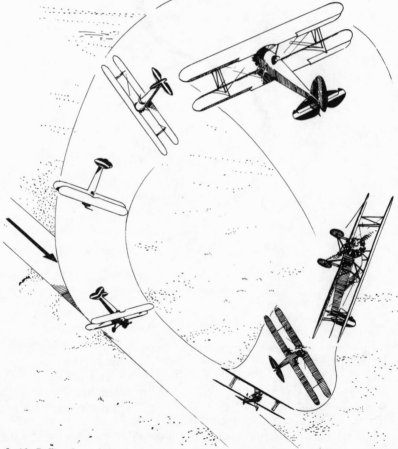

Inside Rolling Loop (outside downward rolling loop identical but with entry from top)

Chinese loop

Here again we have a loop with a single roll, but this time all of the roll takes place in the top half of the loop, so that we fly 2° of roll for every degree of pitch, and this is of course much easier. Termed "Chinese" for no good reason, it was actually devised by the French, who seem to have a great deal of affection for it, if one is to judge by the number of times it appears in their compulsory sequences.

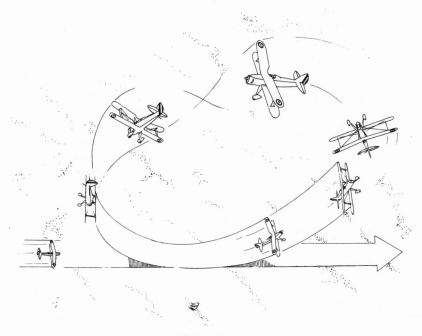

Chinese Loop

Not very pleasing either to fly or to watch, it is really better used as a co-ordination exercise. All these rolling loops need more speed than the standard loop, and in this case the loop is flown normally until the aircraft is just beyond the vertical; and this is important. All three controls are then used harshly to make the machine fly a curved path, erect on the top, and achieving the plane of the inside loop again as the aircraft reaches the vertical dive position, from which the loop is completed normally. Usually one sees only one roll in the Chinese loop.

15   *Outside manoeuvres*

One of the biggest obstacles to flying outside manoeuvres is not the difficulty, disorientation, or even extreme negative *g* involved, but simply the psychological factor of pushing the nose into a steeper and steeper dive, until it is vertical, and still pushing, with the airspeed rising dramatically, the slipstream roaring, and the controls stiffening. Of course one is frightened first time; it would be abnormal to feel otherwise. It doesn't help a great deal to be shown the downward outside loop, because it feels even worse as a passenger than if one is at the controls, so how then can one best cross this hurdle?

It helps if one is relaxed, so before starting to look at the outside loop, it is advisable to practice a little inverted flying. This will also boost one's confidence in the security of the strapping system, which has been properly tightened with outside manoeuvres in mind. It is even more important that one has a good horizon for reference purposes, than is the case in positive figures, so try to pick a day with good visibility for the first attempts.

When considering the loop, it is a good idea to divide it into quarters, and to fly each quarter separately. To gain an idea of what negative *g* feels like, we return to our inverted straight and level exercise, where we raised and lowered the nose, always returning to key point "B". We now repeat the exercise, but we increase the angles until we are going from 45° nose down to 45° nose up, and are achieving between 2 and 3 negative *g* in the process. Make sure that rest periods in normal flight are taken frequently, both from pilot's and engine's point of view. When we are happy with this, dive inverted to a speed of 120 knots (20 knots more than for the inside loop, to allow for inefficient wings and position error), and push steadily and firmly, but not too hard, and in any case not more than 3 negative *g*. Hold the head squarely to the front and do not look "up". One seems to have better peripheral vision under negative *g*, up to the point where "tunnel vision" commences, perhaps due to the eyes swelling up slightly with blood. Some aircraft, the Stampe in particular, have a tendency to tighten up in the outside loop, and it may be necessary to hold back a little on the stick to offset this. It is also difficult to correct any roll or yaw errors at this stage, so having used the inverted slip ball to balance the aircraft in the dive, it is best to clamp the rudder with the feet so that it cannot move. This will also help to keep the feet on the floor of the cockpit, as there is otherwise a tendency for them to float "up" behind the instrument panel, if the aircraft is not equipped with toestraps.

With a starting speed of 120 knots, there is plenty of time to achieve a vertical climb, and as the aircraft approaches the vertical, one can relax the push force, and refer to the wingtips

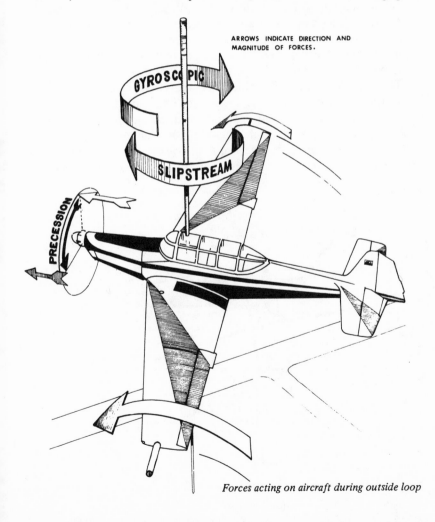

ARROWS INDICATE DIRECTION AND MAGNITUDE OF FORCES.

GYROSCOPIC

SLIPSTREAM

PRECESSION

Forces acting on aircraft during outside loop

to see if the aircraft really is vertical. With a quarter of the loop completed, one may either carry out a recovery from the vertical, or stall turn out, because with the vertical climb established it doesn't matter how we arrived there, we have the capability of stall turning. Be careful on the pullout, because our positive g threshold will be reduced. Having practiced this several times, we can pull up normally to a vertical climb, and then push over the top of an outside loop into a vertical dive, and then pull out.

The negative g involved here is very low, and one really has the impression of flying the aircraft around a curved path. With the very low speed involved, we will need a considerable amount of left rudder to overcome slipstream effects which are trying to turn the aircraft to the right; for we are in normal flight here, albeit at less than one g. In addition, if we pitch forward too quickly, the gyroscopic action of the propeller and engine processes the pitch force through $90°$ in the direction of rotation and causes a further yaw to the right, which can mean that there is not enough left rudder available to keep straight. This can be overcome by more speed, and therefore more rudder power for a given deflection, or a slower pitch rate to reduce the gyroscopic effects, or reduced power to reduce both slipstream and gyroscopics, or one can deliberately put the left wing a little down so that when one

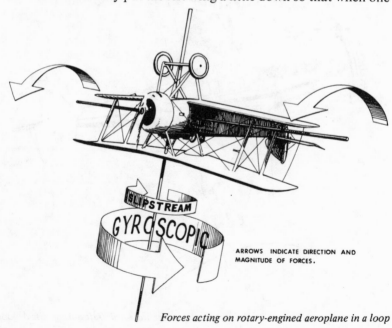

ARROWS INDICATE DIRECTION AND MAGNITUDE OF FORCES.

Forces acting on rotary-engined aeroplane in a loop

runs out of rudder, the first thing that happens is that the wings come back to level, which is exactly what we want! These effects are reversed for a Lycoming engine, and now we begin to realise that the reason for all the rudder on inside loops was due to these same forces. We will see that every time we make a pitch input we must correct with rudder and, vice versa. This is not new information: every fighter pilot in the First World War was familiar with these problems, because of the exaggerated gyroscopic qualities of the rotary engine.

By now, we have achieved three-quarters of the outside loop, in sections: it only remains to fly the quarter from the vertical dive to inverted flight, and this is best done from a normal stall-turn. Instead of pulling out into normal flight after the "cart-wheel turn", we push gently forward as the speed begins to build up. Full power can be left on until the speed approaches 100 knots, and then the throttle setting can be reduced as required. It doesn't matter if the speed gets up to 140 knots, the main thing is, not to panic. Just keep pushing steadily and the nose will come round into inverted flight. It is more important to keep a steady 2 to 3 negative *g* on the accelerometer than to worry about speed, and you should be above 3,000 feet anyway. Under no circumstances should one "chicken out" and pull through.

Outside Loop

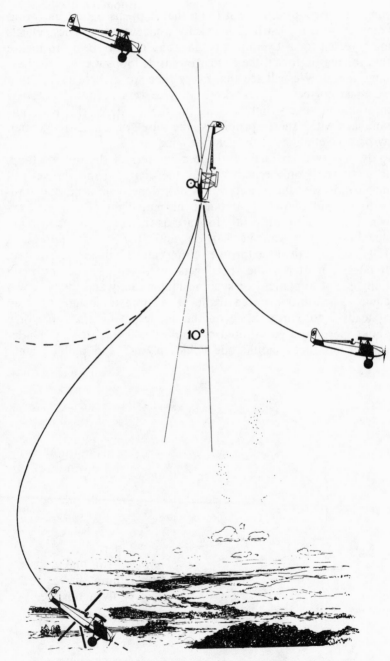

Decision Point – outside manoeuvres

The last point where the figure should be abandoned is 10° beyond the vertical) after that there is no turning back. The first time is the worst, psychologically. Thereafter, it gets easier every time, and eventually one does not need to throttle back on the way down, but can hold the speed under control with *g*, resulting in induced drag, as in the positive loop. By this time we have actually flown two figures, in their component parts, the outside loop and outside stall turn. It is therefore quite easy to fly the complete figure, and in the case of the loop it is better initially to start inverted at the bottom.

The errors in the outside loop are very similar to those found in the inside loop, but there is usually less of a tendency to push too hard at the beginning. Rather, the push is normally too little to start with, and increases as the *g* reduces. Try to remember the errors of the inside loop and it will be apparent that we are still concerned about the negative *g* involved so that we are allowing personal comfort to spoil the shape of the outside loop. Negative *g* is not comfortable, so let us accept that fact: we have to put up with it if we are to fly an accurate figure.

If we push too hard at the top we will stall inverted, in spite of the fact that we are the right way up. It is here that we can have a little respite from negative *g*, so take it easy and fly across the top of the loop. Only when the speed starts to go up on the far side do we start pushing again and on the way down we can easily track along the feature line. It is only too easy to make a roll input in the first quarter of the loop if one is not seated correctly. It may help to use two hands on the stick if this problem persists, merely to get a straight push. The outside loop is usually flown into wind so that the top is more easily made round. The manoeuvre can of course be flown from the top downwards, as can all looping figures.

With the outside loop complete, the outside stall turn will be very easy to fly. It is a little more tricky at first to establish an exact vertical climb, and one's biggest errors will be in terms of unwanted roll input, and incorrect use of rudder. Any wing low correction during the pushing is made with aileron and opposite rudder. When the aircraft is in a true vertical climb, disregard the fact that the entry was inverted, and merely fly a normal stall turn.

Now the spectrum opens up further because we can have a combination of stall turns with various kinds of entry and exit, either for use as turn round or as figures which maintain the

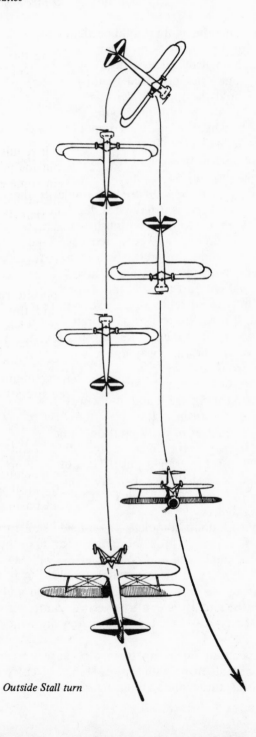

Outside Stall turn

general direction.

We can further expand the repertoire by using the techniques we have learned to fly outside rolls-off-the-top, Cuban 8's, reverse Cuban 8's, and so on. Between ten and twenty per cent is added to all upward outside looping manoeuvres, and we can include all types of rolls to give combination figures.

Outside flickroll

This figure has been left out until now because it requires a good sense of timing and some experience of both outside manoeuvres and inside flick rolls. It is a good thing to gain some experience in inverted spinning before going on to the outside flick roll.

Most aircraft will outside flick more readily than they will in the positive sense, and they can be more reluctant to stop, as the wing is usually more ready to stall abruptly. There is often a greater tendency to buffet if the figure is entered too enthusiastically, with some detriment to the rigging, in the case of a biplane. On some aircraft, absolutely full opposite rudder and full aft stick may be necessary to recover, and this may also require some strength on the controls. Care should be taken to ensure that full control movement is available under negative *g*.

The outside flick roll is most commonly done from inverted flight, and in the case of the Stampe the maximum speed is 75 knots indicated. With full power applied, the aircraft is allowed to accelerate up to this speed, and the stick is smoothly and quickly pushed forward and to one side, whilst the rudder is simultaneously applied opposite to the aileron, so that if the roll is to be to the right, the pilot will apply right aileron, forward elevator, and left rudder at the same time. The machine will then rotate very rapidly, the aileron assisting the roll rate conventionally. With less than 90° to go, the exact position varying for different rate of control application, full opposite rudder and full aft stick (ailerons central) are simultaneously applied. The recovery controls are held hard on until all the rotation has stopped, the engine remaining at full power throughout.

Negative Flick-roll

The nose will be low at the finish, but it must not be raised until the aircraft is properly under control, otherwise control may be lost. If the machine falls into an inverted spin, close the throttle, and the existing control positions will be correct for recovery. This is why inverted spins should be experienced first. It is easier done in a descending line, and more difficult in a climbing line, and it can be done from normal erect flight, in the same way that the erect flick can be done from inverted flight.

If an inverted flick roll fails to stop rotating, and there is an element of confusion, it is very important that the throttle be closed, because the gyroscopic effects may effectively prevent recovery if this is not done. Full power is maintained in the recovery of the precision inverted flick roll primarily to accelerate the aircraft away from a very low speed, and also to provide a good slipstream for the tail surfaces to be able to utilise in recovery.

An important point to appreciate about outside manoeuvres is that because the aeroplane is the right way up with respect to the ground, it does not follow that it must be under positive *g*, and vice versa. Since with the Stampe the propeller turns anti-clockwise as seen from the cockpit; at low speed under positive *g* we will need left rudder, and under negative *g* right rudder. Ally this to gyroscopic effects and one can either eliminate or increase the yaw with pitch. With practice the rudder requirements can be anticipated, but the aircraft should always be flown by feel — the seat of the pants.

Peter Hewitt (Photography) Ltd.

ZLIN 526 in which the author won the European Championship

Arrow Active Mk.2 demonstrates a vertical climb

Air Portraits

The British Team's Pitts Special demonstrates knife flight

Air Portraits

The Pitts Special

The grace of the Monoplane. ZLIN 226 Trener Special

Flight International

Entering a loop.   Stampe SV4B

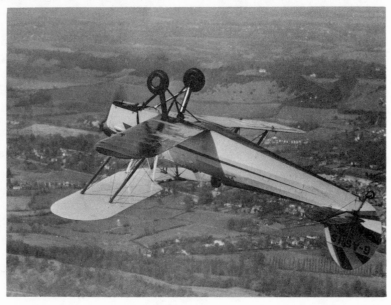

Flight International

Biplane Grace   Stampe SV4B

A Bucker Jungmann looping over Lake Geneva

A Yak 18 PM awaits its turn to fly

Run Up! A Yak 18PS under full power

Low level knife flight: A Bucker Jungmann

Spinks Akromaster

The incomparable Bucker Jungmeister

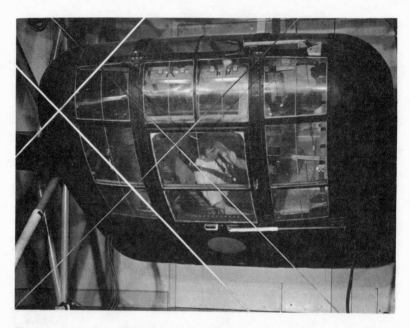

The human centrifuge: Institute of Aviation Medicine, Farnborough

The tracker board in operation

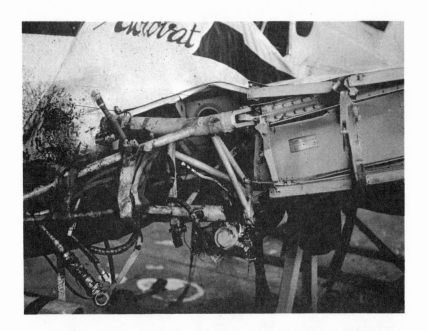

Cause, and . . . .

—effect. Metal fatigue resulted in lower spar boom failure and caused a wing to fold in flight. ZLIN Akrobat, Hullavington, June 1970.

Akrostar

Danish built K.Z.8. only two were made. Powered by Gipsy Major

*Crazy Flying: making the easy look spectacular, the difficult easy, and
never attempting the impossible.*

Peter Hewitt (Photography) Ltd.

"Oh, I have slipped the surly bonds of earth" . . . *ZLIN Akrobat in full flight*

D.H. Chipmunk Mk.22A Bristol Conversion

The author slow rolls a "Super" Tiger Moth

On a stage of infinite breadth and indescribable grandeur – The British Teams
ZLIN Akrobat   Peter Hewitt (Photography) Ltd.

16   *Aresti explained*

Many present day aerobatic pilots glibly talk about Aresti as though it is a style of flying, or consider it as a requirement to fly harsh, sharp angles, losing in the process any real finesse and artistry which they may have had. Aresti is blamed for the present day mechanical approach to aerobatics, and it is certain that there are a large number of pilots who really do not know what it is all about.

I first met Aresti in the days of the Lockheed Trophy, when I peered into the cockpit of his Jungmeister and saw the sequence card adorned with incomprehensible hieroglyphics. For 25 years he had developed his system of building combinations of manoeuvres and assembling them into a dictionary, which we all know today. But originally these little symbols were drawn for his own use, a kind of aeronautical shorthand which acted as an "aide-memoire" in the cockpit during aerobatics. In order to make them easily distinguishable during aerobatic flight he drew some of the figures in an exaggerated way. A good example is the half reverse Cuban drawn thus :

We note that there is a long vertical diving leg, which most people tend to follow religiously, together with its harsh right angle corner at the bottom. But Aresti never meant us to fly like that; certainly he never did it himself to begin with. Agreed, the long diving line is more dramatic, and so is the corner at the bottom in terms of airframe fatigue life.

We have seen several examples of structural failure through making an attempt to fly square corners, and Aresti has been given much of the blame. We should however realise that it is our interpretation which is at fault.

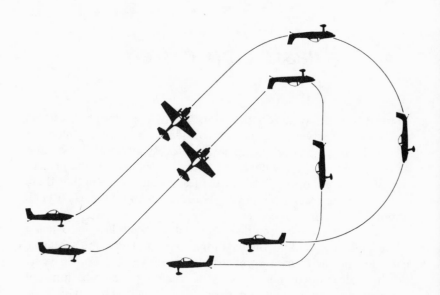

Manoeuvres are not always flown exactly as drawn

Certainly, because the manoeuvres have been drawn out clearly
in the dictionary, we have become obsessed with the requirement
to fly exact 90° and 45° lines; no bad thing from the point of view
of training, but equally one could fly a horizontal 8 with 60°
lines instead of 45°, and in his latest version Aresti provides for
this. Because the system of building composite figures relies on
exact lines and angles, aerobatic flying is in danger of becoming
robot-like, and I have seen many young pilots being unnecessarily
harsh with the aeroplane in the mistaken belief that they were
"flying Aresti". The real contribution Aresti has made lies in
the fact that here we have an international standard which
allows us to judge advanced sequences, with a mathematical basis,
instead of using pure emotion. There is a beauty in symmetric
art, which is also technically correct, and this is what Aresti has
given us. If it has any real failings, apart from our own mis-
interpretation, it is that the system was devised for the Jungmeister, which excelled at flicks but had poor outside looping
performance and vertical rolling capabilities.

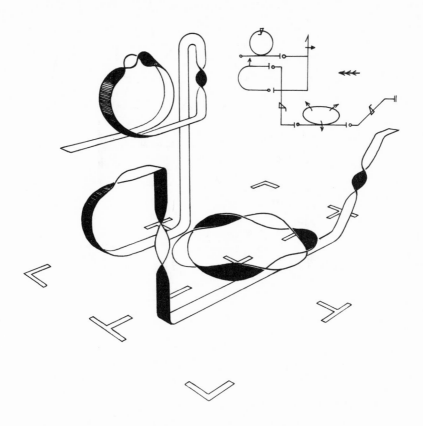

Ribbon interpretation of sample sequence

Before the Aresti "aerocryptographic system" of depicting manoeuvres was devised, pilots at a world championship were faced with a cumbersome and complicated drawing in which the intended path of the aeroplane was shown by "tape-drawing", with the top of the aeroplane shown in white and the underside it black. If is interesting to compare the same sequence using both systems. The Aresti system is so handy to use that we can write down the sequence of an aircraft in flight during its performance, just like shorthand.

Identical Sequences – Aresti and Pre-Aresti

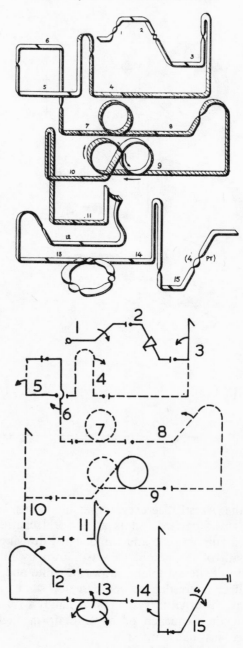

Aresti began by dividing all manoeuvres into families, from 1 to 9, and these are set out below:

Family 1. Lines and angles.

2. Horizontal turns.

3. Vertical turns.

4. Spins.

5. Stall turns.

6. Tail slides.

7. Loops.

8. Rolls.

9. Loops and rolls.

All positive *g* flight is shown by a solid line ∘——————⊣ , while negative *g* flight requires a dotted line ∘———————⊣. Knife flight is thus: ∘— · — · —⊣ . Full rolls are arrows through the line: ∘————↑————⊣, half rolls thus ∘————↗-----⊣ . Flick rolls are equilateral triangles ∘————△————⊣ , while spins are

right angled triangles ; unshaded for inside, shaded for outside.

If all these manoeuvres were cut out of paper, of equal sizes squares, and if the entry and exit lines fitted into the manoeuvres on adjacent squares, the sequence can be flown smoothly, without pause. For example, we know a stall turn follows a loop easily, and it is drawn thus:

However, if we fly a roll-off-the-top followed by a vertical roll, it will not fit:

We can see that all manoeuvres in the dictionary comform to this, and it is deliberate, which makes us realise even more the care involved in producing this system. One is also required to make a distinction between where one figure ends and the next begins, and it is for this reason that one is required to draw a horizontal line before and after each manoeuvre. If Aresti has produced a style at all, it is the drawing of lines, but this does not mean that the flying cannot be smooth, on the contrary, the two complement each other.

We are required to spin about a vertical line, for example, unlike the ordinary spin where the flight path gradually tapers into the vertical, and it may be that we will have to modify our original technique to achieve this, by rolling into the spin with aileron, then using rudder, and lastly pulling the stick back after half a turn, to pull the flight path into the vertical. This is not the perfect spin entry, but it will look perfect from the judges position, and this is what one must think about. Any spin or roll must be centrally placed on any line on which it occurs, so that there is an equal straight line before and after the figure. In the case of an upward roll, the time spent after the roll, on the line, may be three times greater than the time before rolling; but as long as the distances were equal, marks will be high. The roll may be slow, taking almost all of the line, or fast, with a long "lead" and "tail" as they are called; it doesn't matter as long as they are equal.

These criteria have become universally accepted as the norm, but it should be remembered that the rules of each individual competition can modify the basic Aresti concept drastically: "Aresti" is only the foundation of the rules. Each figure in the Aresti dictionary has a "K" factor, which is really a difficulty co-efficient. The harder the figure, the higher the "K" factor; bearing in mind that the dictionary was written around the Jungmeister. Straight and level erect flight has a score of zero! A slow roll is 10 and a loop is 12. In competition scoring, the judge always marks out of 10, and his score is then multiplied by the K factor for the manoeuvre to give the number of points awarded, so if one did a perfect loop, and received a score of 10, since the K factor for the loop is 12, one would have scored 120 aerobatic points. There is also a K factor for positioning, and this will be scored by line judges or by an electronic tracker. In some contests the judges award the score themselves depending on how the sequence has been placed before them.

If one wishes to construct a combination manoeuvre, it can be done very simply using the basic families of figures. For example if one did not know the K value of a vertical 4 point roll, with positive flight entry and exit, thus:

4

we can construct it from the basic shape where K=13, the vertical line on which the roll takes place (K=4), and the basic horizontal 4 point roll (K=11), from which is subtracted the line of the basic figure, in this case a horizontal line (K=0). If we now look in the combination section of the dictionary, the K value for the figure is the same as our sum of 13+4+11 for the three elements, which is 28. It looks complicated at first but one soon gets used to the system.

During a competition one is usually required to construct a free sequence and one is allowed a maximum number of figures, and a maximum total K value, usually 700K in a World Championship. The trick is to select the maximum number of figures, and to ensure that each figure's K value is as near the average as possible. If, at the same time, one selects the simplest possible figures within the rules, one has ensured that mathematically speaking, one has the best chance of a high score.

One is also required to fly an unknown and therefore unpracticed sequence, and it may be that one has never flown a certain figure before. If there are grave doubts as to one's ability to cope with such a manoeuvre, one may be able to fly a slightly modified figure, such that one will receive at least some score, instead of the otherwise inevitable zero. Also one may find oneself about to go out of the box, and one has to decide instantly whether to compromise the figure, with the attendant loss of points, or whether to fly an accurate figure, and accept the penalty for going "outside". Only a detailed knowledge of the system and the rules will allow an instant and correct decision. The "box" itself is made up of two marked axes, 1,000 metres long and 800 metres across, forming a rectangle when perpendicular lines are drawn through their extremities. The height limits are from 100 metres to 1,000 metres above the ground, and the volume of air contained within this cube constitutes the actual aerobatic area, or "box". The whole of the performance must be carried out within this area, which always looks ridiculously small when seen from the air.

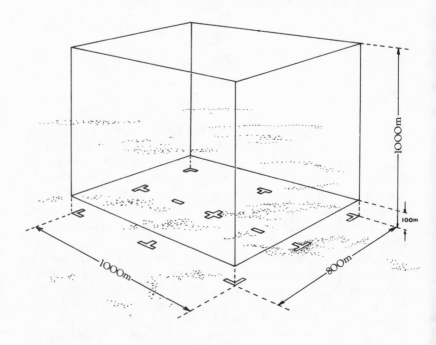

The Box

A cross marks the exact centre of the box, and one is required to balance the performance symmetrically about this point. It is the size of this box which effectively limits the size and performance of aerobatic aeroplanes, and the fairly stiff penalties for going out of the box have probably contributed more to the problems of over-stressing than has the tendency to fly sharp corners for which Aresti has been held responsible. It would do no good to increase the size of the box, though, because although the short term effect would be beneficial, the end result would be to have bigger and more powerful aeroplanes being overstressed!

The best way to remove this problem would be to have the two axes marked, but not to penalise any excursion, except that a balanced performance directly in front of the judges would receive higher scores for presentation.

This form of precision aerobatic flying calls for a very high level of self-discipline, and it is very rare for a competitor to be disqualified for low flying in a world contest.

The Aresti system has a use as an international language, in that, if one writes a sequence down, a Russian or German or Spanish pilot knows exactly what is required, without lengthy explanations and translation. In addition, each family of figures is broken down and each figure has a code number by which it can be positively identified in the dictionary, so that there is no chance of confusion, for example, if we take family 8, we will find that family 8.1. are slow rolls, 8.2 are hesitation rolls, 8.3.1. are inside flick rolls, and 8.3.2. are outside flick rolls, and so on.

If one happens to invent a new manoeuvre, one can go to the basic section of the dictionary and build it up from its component parts, eventually arriving at a K value for it!

The current edition of the Aresti dictionary is the 3rd edition, published in 1967, and it is a "must" for any aerobatic pilot whose goal is the world championship.

There is also a new dictionary in existence, which lists the more outlandish figures, but the original book will cover most requirements. Aresti has many critics, but there is nothing else to replace his work, and it is certain that if he had not produced this system when he did, it would have proved difficult, if not impossible, to score a world championship accurately and fairly.

17   *Fractions of flicks*

To take full advantage of the family of figures in the Aresti dictionary we need to be able to use more than just half slow rolls and half hesitation rolls. These were quite adequate to learn the basic shape of the maneouvre, but now it is time to enlarge the scope. It will therefore be necessary to be able to exchange all "flown" half rolls for flick half rolls; also these half flicks are manoeuvres in their own right. In addition, if we also consider the three-quarter flick rolls, we now have the means of building the "little box" as it is known, and this will bring us into the "B" axis. A full knowledge of these figures will allow us to exploit the box fully, and not just motor back and forth on the main axis.

The two basic half flick forms are in horizontal flight, and consist of the half positive flick from normal flight, and the half negative flick from inverted flight.

In the first case, with the Stampe, a good entry speed is 65 knots, and the manoeuvre goes better to the right, since the flick roll is faster in this direction.

From a low speed, using full power, the aircraft accelerates up to the entry speed. Unlike the full flick, the initiation of the half flick must be very quick, otherwise the aircraft will start to diverge from its intended track before the stall is reached, and this will result in a heading loss. This would not be seen in the full flick roll, because the heading would swing back again in the second half of the roll. Here, however, we are going to stop the roll at the half way point, so any error will be seen. This is the reason for the fast entry, to reduce the amount of divergence.

It follows, too, that the speed must be a little lower, to reduce the stress on the airframe. The manoeuvre is initiated with the simultaneous application of full up elevator and full rudder. Aileron is not required. As the aircraft approaches the inverted position, the rudder is eased a little, but is still deflected in the original sense. At the moment of recovery, the stick is thrust hard forward, and at the same time the throttle is closed, where-upon the aircraft should stop rolling instantly. As soon as the roll stops, open the throttle wide, to prevent any sink. The still deflected rudder will now correct the slight heading error which we have probably not completely eliminated. Another useful dodge is to ease the nose to the left before flick rolling right, but one must tread the tightrope between a heading error and an obvious swing. before the manoeuvre starts. The use of throttle allows the very fast rotation to be stopped instantly; it would otherwise probably overshoot.

The inverted half flick is similarly executed, from inverted flight. Assuming a flick roll to the right, the entry will be similar to the full outside flick, i.e. simultaneous application of full left rudder, stick fully forward, and right aileron, using full power. As the aircraft approaches level flight, the rudder is left on and the stick pulled fully back, at the same time as the throttle is closed. No sooner has the throttle been closed than it is opened wide again, by which time the roll will have stopped with the nose down. As the power comes on the nose can be raised, and the left rudder corrects the inevitable heading error. If this is done in a co-ordinated manner, which will need some practice, the whole manoeuvre will look clean and smooth.

In either of these flicks, if the control application is too slow, or too cautious, the aircraft will describe a half barrel, or "salmon leap" with the wings not stalled, and this will also result in a large heading loss. If these two manoeuvres are flown in a 45° climb, the same principles apply, except that with the nose up, we cannot afford to throttle back. The technique we must use here is to flick as before, but we must start the recovery earlier, since we will not have a power reduction to help us. The speed will be very low at the end of the flick, so we can expect to carry a large amount of rudder in the case of the right hand positive flick from normal flight, and the same will apply in the case of the right hand negative flick from inverted flight. Why, then, do we not fly the flick in the opposite direction? Simply because the flick rate is lower, and the flick is more reluctant to start, thereby producing a large heading error which will be seen by the judges.

It is noticeable that these maneouvres usually go in normal combinations, i.e. the positive flick is from positive flight and the negative flick is from negative flight. However, as with the full flick roll, the half flicks can be done differently in that the positive flick can be flown from a negative line, and so on. It follows that these are awkward manoeuvres to fly, and in this case one would have to push up a little before pulling down into the flick, so as to attempt to keep a reasonable line at the finish. In this case too, one would use all the available aileron to help the roll, because one is being marked on the line one is supposed to hold. We should always bear in mind that the requirement is not to fly what we know is a perfect figure; it is to fly a figure that looks perfect from the judges position, and the two things are very different. During the World Aerobatic Championships in 1964 I flew a modified Cosmic Wind, and I was required to fly an inverted flick roll from an inverted climb of 45°, as part of the unknown sequence. Nobody, to my knowledge had ever done this manoeuvre in a Cosmic Wind, so having watched several experienced pilots spin out of it, I decided to fake it. I pushed the nose up to 45°, kicked the rudder, nudged the stick forward and hit full aileron. Since the aeroplane had a roll rate of 360° per second it was around the roll in a flash, with a bit of yaw and pitch. The judges never having seen the manoeuvre before in a Cosmic Wind, I was given a maximum score, and I hadn't even stalled! I had taken a gamble, and it came off that time. I have also watched Bezàk of Czeckoslovakia fly, and from anywhere on the field other than the judges position, one can see errors. But stand behind the judges and it looks perfect. His is the ultimate demonstration of flying only for the judges; his deliberate errors are designed to look better than a correct manoeuvre!

An area where the half flick is very useful is in a vertical diving line, following a three-quarter loop. Normally one sees a positive half flick with an inside loop, and vice versa, but, as before, we can interchange the loops and flicks. Here we must be careful, because if we delay too long in our attempts to round off the loop, and to establish a good vertical line before the flick, the airspeed may be too high to flick safely. Again one is faced with compromise; I personally pause for a fraction of a second, just long enough to establish the beginning of a line in the judges eyes, and then flick. Although the lines before and after will not be equal. I usually find that the judges are so relieved to see a clean flick in a Stampe that they do not deduct marks! Of course, in a Pitts or Akrostar, we can draw the correct line before flicking.

Another problem which arises is very similar to the heading problem encountered in the horizontal flick, but this time it is a pitch error, where the aircraft starts to respond to the pitch input before the stall occurs, and is deflected from its vertical flight path. To overcome this one must "lay off" the amount of expected displacement, so that when the flick occurs the aircraft comes on to line. In the three-quarter inside loop and half positive flick roll downwards, , the flick is initiated just before the aircraft gets to the vertical, so that the final line is correct; because it is the final line which catches the judge's eye.

We can now develop this figure into a three-quarter diving flick roll which will give us a 90° direction change, and the same considerations apply, except that if we make an error in pitch at the start, it will be seen as an error in yaw in the vertical dive after the flick. In this manoeuvre it is better to lead with rudder, so that one can approach the vertical more closely at the start. At the 180° point in the roll, the aircraft will be yawed off line, but this does not matter because we are still rotating. When it stops at 270°, the aircraft will be slightly on its back, but the whole figure will have been cleaner. There is usually no problem in stopping a vertical diving flick roll in the normal manner, i.e. full opposite rudder followed by elevator, since the airspeed is increasing all the time. Although full power is used to initiate the flick, it is a good idea to throttle back once the rotation starts, to give oneself more time to judge the recovery.

With the 270° downward flick understood, the inverted flick roll being materially the same, one can precede it by a quarter vertical roll, pulling or pushing into level flight prior to executing our flick roll. This will trace a "doorframe" effect in the sky, across the major axis, and is known as a "little box". If we fly one of these combinations at each end of the axis, in the first case we will be displaced from the main axis, and we use the second one to get back on to it. Now we are beginning to use the "box". The climbing flick rolls need a fine sense of timing, and are not really suited for the Stampe, so now we must look at more advanced types.

A common manoeuvre in recent competitions is the three-quarter vertical climbing inside flick, with a push or pull to level flight, so let us consider the figure with the Zlin 526 in mind. Since the propeller rotation is the same as the Stampe, we will find that the flick, as before, goes better to the right, so if, for example, we need to fly level in normal flight at the top of the manoeuvre, our planned exit direction will be on our right as we run in for the figure. I have seen pilots using more and more speed and *g* in an attempt to retain enough airspeed to fly off the top of the flick, and the only result of this in the end was an overstressed aeroplane. However, it is not such a difficult figure if we use our heads. A speed of 250 km/hr is plenty prior to pulling up to the vertical: most Zlins are calibrated in kilometres per hour so we will use

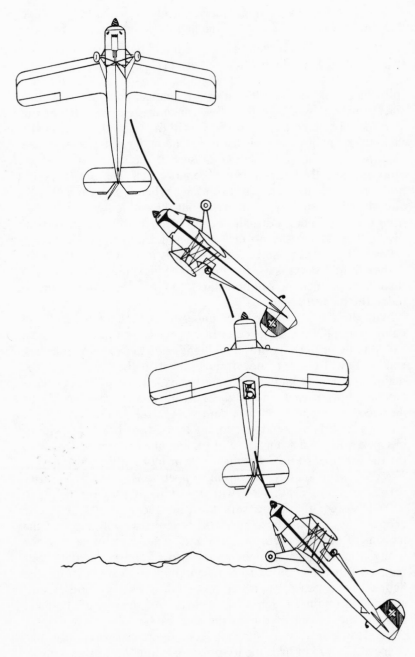

Vertical three-quarter Flick – pitch error allowed for

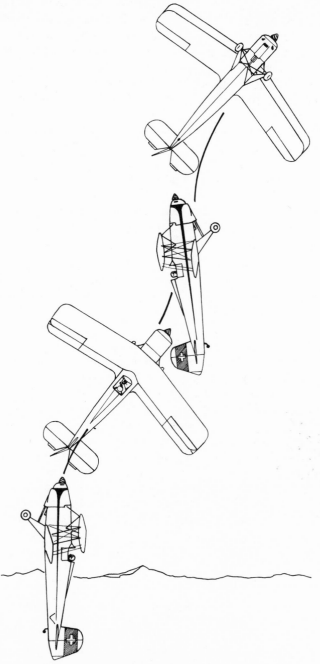

Vertical three-quarter Flick — failing to anticipate pitch error

these units. As we pull up, using about 4*g*, we drop the right wing slightly, and this starts the aeroplane inclining to the right. The pitch is held a few degrees before the vertical to establish the line and to allow the airspeed to decrease to a safe value, and the flick is entered by leading with rudder and bringing the stick straight back. As soon as the flick starts, centralise the stick; the roll will continue, but with less pitch and yaw than normal, and the rate of speed decay will be less.

As the 270° mark is approached, and identified by looking left for the main axis, about half left rudder and slight forward stick will be needed to stop the rotation, still with plenty of speed left. The fact that the aeroplane pitched up slightly before it stalled on the way up, resulted in the flightpath becoming truly vertical, and our initial right wing down technique, though not enough to be seen by the judges, was sufficient to tip the aircraft forwards at the end of the flick, making the push into level flight that much easier.

If we had wanted to fly off inverted, we would have dropped the left wing on the way in. It will be seen that there is no need to abuse the aeroplane when a little common sense and pre-planning will suffice. On all vertical flick rolls, it is best to leave full power applied throughout, as we are still trying to achieve the basic requirements of an established line before and after the rotation, and if power is reduced, the line after the flick will be lost.

If one's aeroplane flicks better in one direction, it may be that one will have to plan the entire sequence to allow for this to happen. Sometimes it happens that any crosswind will favour this, in which case one's positioning problems are very much reduced. On the other hand, a situation may arise where one has no choice but to flick in the opposite direction, so it follows that all flick rolls should be practised to both left and right. One is not rigidly tied to the two axes, as long as the whole sequence is balanced about the centre of the two axes. There is usually no specific requirement to flick right or left, except that sometimes, to prevent a 180° direction loss with its attendant zero score, one has to flick "against" the propeller.

18   *The vertical roll*

If the slow roll was the foundation stone of basic aerobatic flying, then the vertical roll can be said to be the key to world championship flying. In such a contest there will probably be more variations on the vertical roll than on any other manoeuvre. Basically very simple, in fact it causes a lot of problems, particularly if it is not well understood and practised from the beginning. Earlier, we placed a lot of emphasis on establishing the vertical quickly and accurately when we were learning stall turns, and it is here that the benefit of those early lessons will be realised. Each aeroplane will have its own idiosyncrasies, but the principles are generally the same. The aim is to achieve the vertical climb, from positive or negative flight, with the maximum possible speed remaining. It will follow that from a given entry speed there will be one value of *g* only for the particular aeroplane at that moment which will allow it to attain the vertical without losing unnecessary speed. If the entry is too tight or too slack, the ensuing roll will suffer. Each aeroplane will have a slightly different attitude in the vertical climb so that when full aileron is applied, the tail should not describe a circle about the rolling axis: the roll must be straight and true. On some types full aileron is not necessary, and this must be regulated so that the roll does not have the appearance of undue effort.

Once the roll has started I find it easiest to look at one wingtip as it races around the horizon; if the horizon is apparently moving up and down relative to the wingtip, I know that the vertical was not properly established. It is a good idea to look out in the opposite direction to the roll, because although it seems an unnatural thing to do, it does allow the feature on which the roll has to stop to be picked up early, instead of seeing it suddenly materialise from behind the wing.

If the roll is not absolutely vertical, one can use elevator and rudder to force it into the vertical, but since there is some interaction between these one will see the results of an elevator input in yaw, and a rudder input in pitch! At this stage, a fast rolling aeroplane has some of the properties of a gyroscope! From the

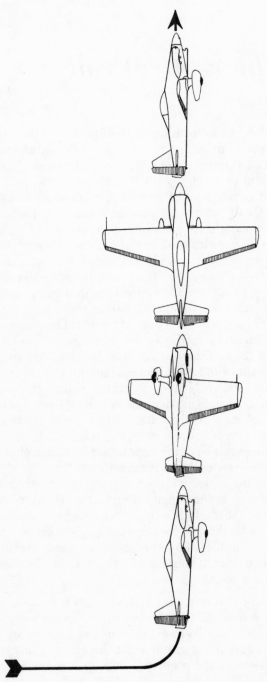

Vertical Roll

ground, the aeroplane would adopt a corkscrew path through the air while these corrections were in progress, so it is obviously better to get it right in the first place.

In addition, if one starts applying rudder and elevator in the vertical roll, it is effectively the same as extending airbrakes, i.e. a resulting loss of speed. Should the roll not be properly vertical, e.g. the pullup has been made short of the vertical, at the 90° and 270° points, the wings will be noticeably yawed, and since 90° and 270° rolls are almost as common as 180° and 360° rolls, it is very important to get it right from the beginning. Prior to the World Championships in 1962, Toth of Hungary practiced for over 70 hours on vertical rolls alone, such was the importance attached to the manoeuvre. Nobody was surprised when he won!

Generally, aircraft roll better "with" the engine, so that the Zlin goes better to the right and the Pitts to the left. Because of the side thrust which results from the deflected ailerons, rudder has to be used in the direction of roll, towards the top of the manoeuvre, in order to keep it straight. This results in a sideslip away from the direction of roll, which can be modified a little by slipstream effects, and of course by errors in the roll. If the roll has been straight, this sideslip is at its highest when the ailerons are centralised at the completion of the roll, and the result of this is that the aeroplane is reluctant to stall turn in the same direction as we have just done the roll.

Even with the engine still at full power, in the case of the Zlin, after a right hand roll, the machine will not go cleanly to the right, but instead will stall turn quite well to the left. The Pitts, with its very high power to weight ratio, is less affected, the predominant factor being propeller slipstream.

At the top of a vertical roll, the aeroplane is slightly reluctant to stall turn cleanly; is more prepared to accept a pull through 180° into the vertical; but much prefers a push through 180°. During the initial attempts at the vertical roll, therefore, it is better to push forward to recover, in fact, if one makes one quick forward stick input, and then returns the stick to neutral, the aircraft will very often pitch over the top with no fuss at all.

Many aircraft tend to lose the vertical line after the roll, in that they pitch forward about 5°, so on these types the stick must be eased back when the roll stops, prior to exiting from the man-oeuvre.

Orientation is always a problem, especially in poor visibility when there may not be a distinct horizon, and this is where it pays

Totem Pole

to have an aeroplane which has some inherent stability and feel, such as the Zlin. In this aircraft one receives so much information from the seat of the pants and feedback in terms of feel through the controls, that one can continue the roll fairly accurately even if one has run into a patch of cloud! It will be obvious, from that statement, that timing plays a very large part in the vertical roll, indeed in all aerobatics. In an aircraft like the Zlin, one received a great deal of information from the above sources, but with a neutrally stable aircraft like the Akrostar, where one relies mostly on visual cues, one would be in some degree of trouble if there was a deterioration in visibility.

When learning vertical rolls in these two types, one would no doubt learn faster in the Akrostar, but the mastery of the manoeuvre in a Zlin is a real accomplishment, which will be of much more value in the future. With a good feel for the aeroplane, if one is caught out in bad visibility, one can look back over the tailplane and watch the axes revolving, knowing just by feel and timing that the machine is rolling straight.

There are many variations of the vertical roll, including the reverse roll, where one half rolls one way, then half rolls back the other. In this case, the first half roll should be against the engine, so that the aeroplane can roll "with" the engine torque when aileron rolling power has almost gone.

Aresti permits the inclusion of vertical rolls in stall turns, tail slides and half loop and half roll combinations as well as vertical rolls in their own right. Consuming a large area of sky, they are one of the most impressive of manoeuvres, and are often used to start a free style sequence. When one has practiced the vertical roll until it is almost second nature, one can then build on it.

As an example, to open my free style routine in the Pitts Special, I start on the "B" axis, diving towards the judges, at VNE; which is followed by a pullup to the vertical, a four point vertical climbing roll to the left, followed by an inside flick roll to the right and stall turn left. On the diving line I have an outside flick roll right and an aileron roll left, pulling out tail to the judges. It is only years of work on the vertical roll which allows us to flick roll cleanly off the top, and still have speed to stall turn. With practice, these manoeuvres can be flown by anyone.

19   Advanced spinning and falling leaf

The flat spin

Any spin whose fuselage angle is less than 45° from the horizontal is defined as a flat spin; however there is a world of difference between a spin which qualifies for this distinction by one or two degrees, and the full blooded true flat spin with the nose near the horizon, and a rate of rotation so fast that the ground is just a blur. Apart from the flat attitude and high rotation rate, the flat spin has another important characteristic, and that is its very low height loss per turn.

Normally the flat spin is entered from a normal stable spin, and in this case the flat spin is usually stable following a smooth transition. One can also enter the flat spin direct, say from the top of a slow outside loop. Whether or not the flat spin will be immediately stable depends on the sink rate achieved prior to applying rudder, and on the characteristics of the aeroplane generally. It is typical of flat spins that they take several turns to stop, so in spite of the low height loss per turn it is advisable not to get too low.

The aircraft will flat spin best "with" the propeller, so on the Zlin this will be to the right. The engine is used as an extra control in the flat spin, and its gyroscopic properties are made to work for us. With a propeller which turns anticlockwise when seen from the cockpit, as in the Zlin; if we yaw the aircraft to the right, the yawing force is taken 90° in the direction of engine rotation, and appears as a nose up pitching force, whose magnitude depends upon the rpm. Of course, it also depends upon C.G., momentum of the engine/propeller combination, and spin rate. Of these, the only one we can adjust in flight is spin rate, and this can not only be done by increasing power to yaw faster, but also by applying outspin aileron. This has the effect of applying additional rudder due to the downgoing aileron, as well as reducing the wing tilt, which we see as bank in the direction of the spin. This bank is really roll, and if we reduce it, the spin energy, since it cannot be destroyed is transferred into yaw. The result is a flat spin in both pitch and bank, with an increased rotation rate, and a smaller flight path helix around the wind axis. What we see from the ground is best compared with a falling sycamore leaf in autumn.

Many aerobatic aeroplanes will not flat spin because the C.G. is so far forward that the aerodynamic restoring force from the tail-plane and elevator overcomes the gyroscopic and aerodynamic factors which are acting in favour of the spin: the result is then an oscillatory, but normal spin.

If we look at the erect flat spin from inside a Zlin 526, we will see that it can be entered from any position which will permit a normal spin. If we first establish a normal spin to the right, and wait for it to stabilise, we will note that it is faster than the left hand spin, with the nose a little higher, about 50° to 60°, and we have about 5° to 10° of bank to the right. If we now apply full left aileron, still keeping the stick back, the nose will come up

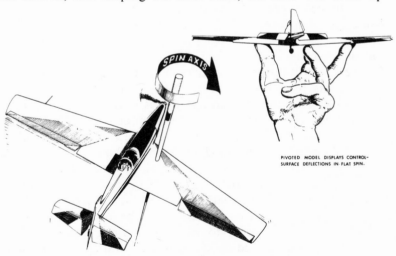

Flat Spin, ZLIN 526A

to about 45° to 40°, with a faster rotation and less bank. Technically, we have a flat spin. However, let us go further. If we now apply full power, the nose comes up dramatically to about 10° below the horizon, and we really start to rotate, but the vertical descent has now slowed. To complete the requirements for the flat spin, still with full power and full aileron, push the stick fully forward! By now the nose will be on or above the horizon in a fully developed flat spin in the best sense of the term. The reason for this forward stick is thought to be that it blanks off the fin and rudder, which are now moving so fast that they are tending to slow the spin.

To recover, as one would expect, one merely reverses the operation. Stick back, throttle closed, ailerons neutral, and when the aircraft stabilises full left rudder and stick forward. It will take up to $2\frac{1}{2}$ turns to stop, and it will feel longer, so don't panic; just give the recovery action time to work.

It is easy to get caught out flat spinning, so having done it, and described it here, let me say that I do not personally use the manoeuvre! The Zlin requires a great deal of care in the spin, but as with any aeroplane, it does not do to take ¡any' liberties. All Zlins have a white spin spot painted on the instrument panel so that the stick can be aimed at it during the recovery thus en-suring ailerons neutral. But the most important thing in spinning a Zlin is to make sure that the throttle is fully closed in recovery, to reduce gyroscopic force.

The inverted spin

For years an atmosphere of alarm has surrounded the inverted spin. It has been banned in the Service, and has the dubious reputation of having claimed many lives in the past. So perhaps the time has come to try and put it in its proper perspective, since it is used widely in international contest work. It has been one of the most widely misunderstood figures in aerobatics, and much has been written about it in the past, not all of it accurate.

To begin with, apart from the fact that the aeroplane is upside down, there is nothing remarkable about the inverted spin. If we look back to our wild character riding on the inverted belly of the aeroplane it will be easier to see what is going on. Since most normal spins are entered from a slow deceleration into the stall, our hero will want to do the same here, so with the extended stick protruding through the belly of the aeroplane in the firm grasp of our intrepid rider, let us see what happens in a spin to the right. We know that the stick comes back slowly until the stall is approached, whereupon right rudder and full back stick are then applied, and the aircraft starts to spin to the right, Because the wings are less efficient in the inverted attitude, it may help to assist the roll with some right aileron as the spin commences. Meanwhile, our inverted pilot will see the stick going forward as the speed

Simplified inverted spin entry and recovery

falls, until at the moment of stall, left rudder is applied, followed by stick forward and to the right. The aircraft is now in a right hand inverted spin as seen from outside, but the pilot will see a yaw to the left, and a roll to the right. This is the big difference in the inverted spin; the roll and yaw are in opposite directions, however, the turn indicator always tells the truth, and shows a yaw to the left.

Spinning: Needle indicates direction of yaw whether erected or inverted.
In this case right rudder is required to recover. In the spin ignore all slip indications

So that there is no possibility of confusion regarding direction for an inverted spin, I usually stipulate "spin with left foot" or "spin with right foot", as otherwise argument can arise: actually, it all depends on the observers point of view!

The recovery is again straightforward. From the exposed belly of the aircraft, the machine appears to be in a normal spin to the right: so, to recover, we apply left rudder and push the stick forward, at the same time centralising the ailerons. These actions seen from the cockpit would be full right rudder, and stick fully back with ailerons neutral.

It is all quite simple when seen from this point of view, and in fact once this is realised, and one is used to seeing the roll and yaw in opposite directions, the inverted spin is seen in its proper perspective.

Although the inverted spin is conventionally entered from a slow deceleration in inverted flight there is nothing to prevent the spin from being initiated from erect flight, and of course the erect spin can also be entered from inverted flight. Two methods apply here, both with the same purpose in view, i.e. to achieve a vertical flightpath as soon as possible. In the case of the inverted spin from erect flight, the aircraft is brought to the point of the positive stall, whereupon the stick is snatched back to promote an instant normal *g* break. As the aircraft drops, full forward stick, and full rudder with opposite aileron are applied, and the aircraft tucks under and starts to spin inverted. The other method is to bring the aircraft almost to the point of stall, and to roll it in, say with right aileron, followed by forward stick, and as the bank approaches 90°, left rudder! Hardly the standard entry, but it does allow a stable spin to develop rather earlier than it would otherwise do.

In both erect and inverted spins, the slip ball merely shows the sideslip, and this is not of special significance to the aerobatic pilot, so for competition work it can be ignored. As in the erect spin, if in doubt, centralise the controls and close the throttle, remembering to give your every action chance to work before abandoning it.

In all spinning, we must make sure that there is nothing to restrict control movement, for example rudder restriction due to partially applied brakes in a Chipmunk. Most aircraft will recover more easily from the inverted spin than from the erect spin, because the fin and rudder have access to clean laminar air which allows maximum elevator and rudder effectiveness without the blanking which can apply in the erect spin.

There is another point to be borne in mind with the inverted spin, and that is that the rotation is usually faster than in the erect spin, probably for the very reason that the tail section is not blanked. This means that one very often overshoots the intended point, not because the spin is hard to stop, but because it is rotating so fast that our anticipation is at fault, and here again is a source of adverse comment against the manoeuvre, If one has to do more than one turn of an inverted spin it is best to slightly reduce rudder and elevator after the first turn, and this will keep the rotation steady, at the expense of increasing airspeed and greater height loss. Of course, there comes a limit if one does this where the aircraft stops spinning and goes into an inverted spiral dive — but that is not a spinning problem! During all forms of spinning one may expect considerable altimeter lag, so do not place too much faith in the indicated altitude! In the spin the ground never appears to be very close until the last few hundred feet, when it approaches very rapidly indeed, so always recover with plenty of height to spare.

Finally, if one makes any errors in the recovery from the erect spin, for example pushing the stick forward, but forgetting to apply opposite rudder, a very fast, steep spin can develop which looks rather like an inverted spin to a pilot who is not familiar with the inverted spinning characteristics of his aeroplane. If he then takes recovery action for what he thinks is an inverted spin all he will do is to put it back into a normal erect spin. If you practice both, there will be no confusion, and you will be a better, safer, pilot!

Inverted Spin

The inverted flat spin

A form of spinning not widely used, it is however, occasionally seen in a World Championship. Although I would personally not use it, it is perhaps a good thing to experience when one has accumulated a lot of spinning time. Again, it is less dangerous than the erect flat spin, because, in common with the standard inverted spin, it recovers more easily, for the same reasons.

As in the erect flat spin, the entry to the flat condition is usually via the stable spin. Let us therefore look at the inverted flat spin in the Pitts Special, which is probably the fastest rotation that we are likely to see anywhere. As we have seen, we can enter the inverted spin from several different manoeuvres; the normal method being a slow inverted deceleration, although we could half loop to the inverted or enter as a push down manoeuvre from erect flight.

Extreme attitude of inverted flat spin PITTS S1–S

The inverted spin will be entered with right rudder and forward stick, the use of ailerons being unnecessary in view of the symmetrical wings. Having reached a stable condition in the inverted spin, we apply outspin aileron, i.e. right aileron, always remembering that in the erect spin outspin aileron is opposite to rudder, whilst inverted spins require aileron in the same direction as rudder to qualify as outspin. A word with our Genghis Khan character will resolve any confusion here! As the outspin aileron goes on, the spin flattens out and speeds up, but with the application of full power the results are awe inspiring! The nose goes up, above the horizon, so that we can see daylight "above" the top wing! The wings are absolutely level, and the rotation exceeds 400° per second! There is no point looking at the ground or the horizon, nothing can be identified, in fact it is so fast that it is hard to define the direction. The enormous gyroscopic force provided by the engine in this tiny aeroplane is responsible for the high rotation, but I do not care to subject the engine bearers to the high forces involved, so I do not use it in competition. The g loads in the cockpit are quite small, but one might not be surprised to find they are considerably higher on the extremities of the aircraft. The recovery is satisfyingly quick: as soon as one throttles back and centralises ailerons, the machine drops into a normal inverted spin, from which recovery is straightforward and immediate. It is a safe enough figure, provided the C.G. is inside the aft limit!

The falling leaf
Here we are taking a look back into the dawn of aeronautical history for the "falling leaf" is almost as old as the aeroplane. Never used in modern competition, it is worthwhile learning what it is and how to do it, not only, like Mount Everest, "because it is there", but because it requires a sensitive touch and razor sharp timing if it is going to work; and both of these are important factors in our modern flying. So rather than scoffing at such an ancient manoeuvre, let us look at it more closely.

It consists of a series of incipient spins, each checked almost instantly, only to have the direction reverse, and then checked again, and so on. If we are too slow, the aircraft really will spin; too fast and we will just wallow downwards in a semi-stalled condition. Since the engine is throttled well back, we will need considerable altitude, approximately 200 feet per "leaf". The manoeuvre is best done when pointing directly at the judges, so

Falling leaf

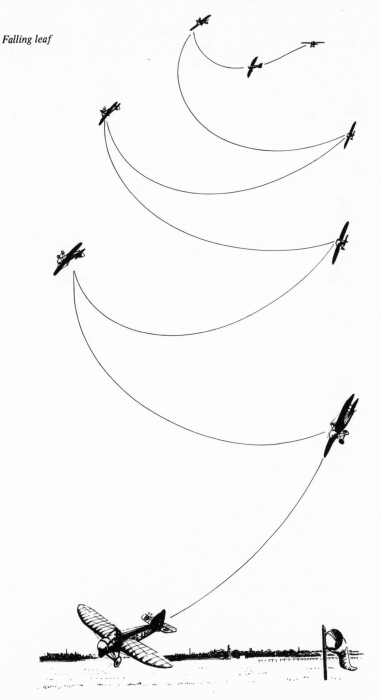

that the shape can best be seen. One will appreciate instantly why it is so called, because its behaviour is exactly like a large leaf, swooping from side to side.

It is best flown with a biplane, and a low wing loading biplane at that; and for the first time, a Tiger Moth will beat any other aeroplane! Engine rotation tends to make the leaves faster in one direction, and this must be compensated for by the pilot.

The technique is to bring the aircraft to the point of stall, and apply pro-spin controls quickly. As the wing goes down, apply full opposite rudder and forward stick, whereupon the incipient spin will stop. Before the speed can build up, keep the rudder on and pull the stick back, which will precipitate an incipient spin in the opposite direction; as the wing goes down, again apply full opposite rudder and forward stick, and so on. One will soon learn to develop a rhythm which will suit the individual aeroplane, and the machine will descend in a graceful series of sweeping arcs, making slow forward progress over the ground. It is even more spectacular done into the wind, with zero groundspeed. The manoeuvre is stopped by simply not pulling back at the end of a leaf, whereupon it will accelerate and regain flying speed.

20 *Wind and its effects*

When an aeroplane is in flight, it operates within the mass of air that supports it, whether that mass is stationary or moving. If it were otherwise, most of the problems of navigation would be resolved. In a sense, we too have a problem of navigation, for we have to fly a series of pre-planned and intricate routes through the air, and they must be the same, whether the wind is blowing or not, with respect to the ground.

Now when we realise that the ratio between the windspeed and the speed of the aircraft is 1:5, we know we are going to have a problem. In effect, we are going to have to manoeuvre the aircraft inside a frame 1,000 metres long by 800 metres wide, and fly precise geometric shapes in relation to the fixed axes on the ground, whilst continually moving the overall sequence in a given direction at up to 25 mph. There are not many computers which could handle that problem plus all the other parameters involved!

In addition, the wind strength and direction will probably change within the vertical confines of the "box", so that one is continually making adjustments. As if this were not enough, we may have to put up with a wind 30° off the main axis, which will drift our sequence either towards or away from the judges. If we lay off drift in the time honoured navigational manner, we will lose points for accuracy, and if we do not do anything we will eventually go out of the box. I have watched Bezàk, the first World Champion, operating in a crosswind, and the technique he used was to sideslip with wings level; this was changed from erect to inverted, maintained in the vertical, and adjusted for the direction and strength of the wind. In effect, it seemed that the wind had ceased to blow, and the next competitor obviously thought so too, because he started, full of confidence, only to be blown out of position before he had flown half a dozen manoeuvres.

In a world championship, the maximum permitted wind strength is 10 metres per second. It became a standing joke at Hullavington during the world championships in 1970 that the wind speed was 9·8, gusting 9·9 metres per second! The wind, needless to say, was blowing!

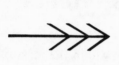

Aeroplane climbing in vertical attitude,
drifting in strong wind

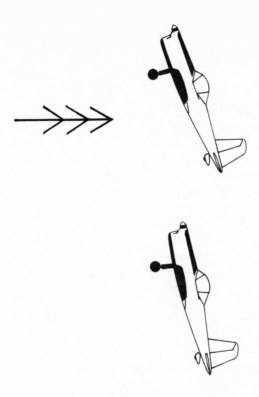

*Aeroplane climbing vertically –
compensating for wind*

Aircraft with high operating speeds are less affected by wind than the slower types, and they are able to hold well into wind. The capabilities of such aircraft as the Yak 18 are indicated by the fact that nearly all their manoeuvres are flown into wind, with only the occasional figure to take them back to the downwind end of the "box".

Normally the judges mark on "flightpath". That is to say, they expect to see a vertical track through the air, as opposed to a vertical aircraft attitude. Of course, in zero wind, both of these coincide, so again it is the strength and direction of the wind that concerns us. In the case of a stall turn flown into the wind, the manoeuvre must be tilted forwards slightly at first, then more and more as the airspeed falls, to maintain the vertical track. At the moment of stall turning, the aircraft must come back to the vertical plane for the "cartwheel", and then it must be allowed to go on to its back a little, again to hold the vertical line. As speed builds up in the dive, the displacement can be reduced.

Now this is quite straightforward in the case of the stall turn, but suppose we want to fly a vertical 90° roll, and then stall turn? Again we tilt the aircraft forward to track vertically, but as we roll, the wings become tilted, so that at the 90° mark, although the track is still vertical, the aircraft is obviously yawed, and this will lose marks. It looks like a "heads I win, tails you lose" situation, in favour of the judges! However, we can fix that. As the roll approaches 90°, say, during a right hand roll, if we apply smooth left rudder just before the roll stops, we can yaw the aircraft so that it points straight up: also, with left rudder, we are sideslipping vertically to the right, and therefore still tracking vertically! Not only that, but with right sideslip established we are set up for a right stall turn, yawing into wind, and therefore using the wind to improve the shape of the figure, since stall turns sometimes have a tendency to fly around a curve instead of pivoting around the C.G.

Before we lose ourselves in self-congratulation, let us now consider a full vertical roll, again into the wind. If we tilt the line of the roll so that we track vertically, the wings will be yawed at the 90° and 270° points. If we correct on rudder to align the wings with the horizon at these points the tail of the aircraft will barrel badly, so what can we do here?

The real answer is not to fly flightpath in the roll, but to place the aircraft in the true vertical attitude. The roll may then be carried out cleanly; to be sure, it will drift, but not much during

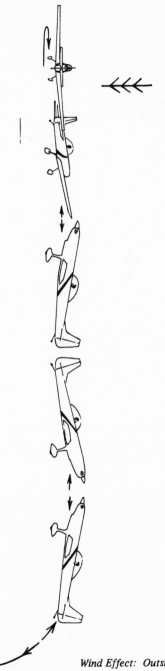

Wind Effect: Outside stall-turn, corrected

Wind Effect: Outside stall-turn, uncorrected

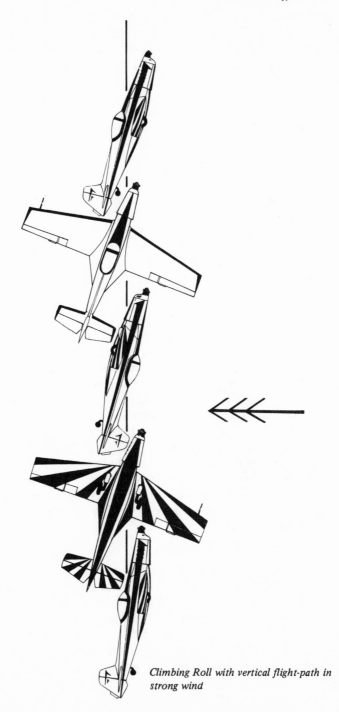

*Climbing Roll with vertical flight-path in
strong wind*

the duration of the roll, and as soon as the roll stops, we can start to fly flightpath again, by tilting the aircraft forward.

Another factor to be borne in mind is that although the judges say at the briefing that .hey are going to mark on flightpath alone, in practice this is not always so. Because the manoeuvres look so awkward if one flies a precise vertical flightpath in a strong wind, it is often better to compromise between attitude and flightpath. With experience, one gets to know the balance between the two which actually scores most points.

When composing a sequence, one usually places certain manoeuvres to allow the wind to help to shape them, so that eight sided loops are usually flown into wind, as indeed are most looping figures, although they may be less critical. An important manoeuvre to place relative to the wind is the tail slide, which we will find needs to be "tipped" before the backward flightpath, and by careful use of the wind the true vertical flightpath can be maintained.

Generally, if the vertical flightpath can be achieved without compromising the manoeuvre, this is the best solution.

Occasionally, in a compulsory programme, one is faced with a looping figure downwind, and here one must really "fly out" the top of the loop to preserve the circular shape, which would otherwise be distorted. Radii are increased downwind, so that it is inadvisable to stall turn with the wind if one is working the "B" axis, as this would destroy the shape of the figure; rather one would "cartwheel" into the wind, thus greatly improving the shape. At the same time, knife edge loops will have added dramatic effect as the wind widens them out. This also applies to a half loop from a vertical climb to a vertical dive, where the wind can produce either a pleasing radius, or a pivot on a spot about the lateral axis, depending on whether one has the wind on the tail or on the nose during the manoeuvre.

Perhaps the most difficult manoeuvres to fly in a strong wind are the figures of 8. If we take a normal inside-outside horizontal 8, otherwise known as a "pair of spectacles"; if the wind is strong one is literally in some danger of making a spectacle of oneself! Starting into wind we are required to fly an inside loop until we are in an inverted 45° dive (flightpath again), and then to push around an outside loop until we achieve a 45° erect dive, with a recovery to level flight.

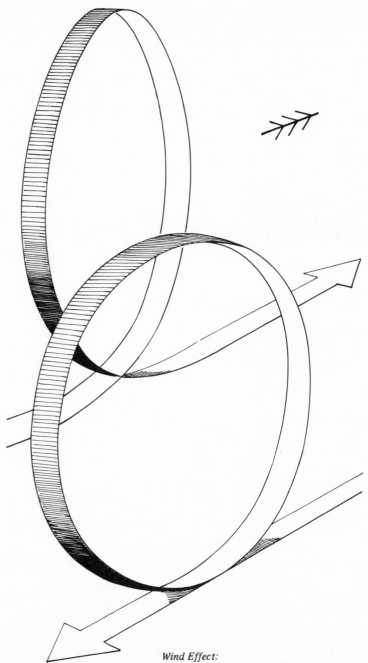

Wind Effect:
Upper drawing – Wind compresses top of loop and impairs shape
Lower drawing – Wind extends top of loop and improves shape

During the early stages of the inside loop the pull must be quite gentle, otherwise the wind will tighten the radius, but as we pass the vertical climb we must start to pull tighter, for now the wind is behind us, pushing us along. We pull quite quickly to the dive angle of about 50° or even more, because the wind will shallow the line, decreasing this dive angle slightly as the speed builds up and the wind effect is reduced. A hard push at the bottom, because our groundspeed is high (remember this figure is flown only with reference to the ground, as indeed they all are). Maintain this high negative *g* until we are through the vertical climb, and then slow the pitch rate right down, for now we are coming into wind again, and our groundspeed is almost zero. Slowly, very slowly, over the top, trying to imagine a perfect arc in the sky, and down to perhaps 35° to start with: the wind will steepen the line for us. As the speed rises, gently steepen the altitude to 40°, to maintain the 45° flightpath. I always try to imagine an arrow on the ground to give me wind direction, because good adjustment for wind will make all the difference.

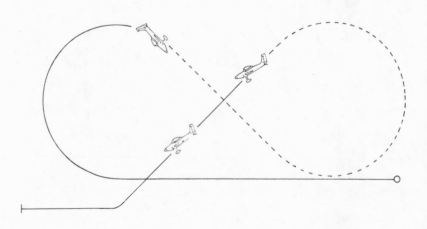

Horizontal Eight

Another effect of wind is to cause the pilot to motor upwind to regain position, and to rush those manoeuvres which are flown in a downwind direction. This means that not only does the aircraft lose the flow and rhythm which are an integral part of aerobatics, but it also loses speed, which can only be recovered at the cost of height. Wind often brings turbulence which not only causes drag because the controls have to be deflected to correct the path of the aeroplane, but also brings the risk of an overstress, so that the pilot cannot use as much *g* as he would normally do. A strong wind can, in combination with a particular sequence, make a world champion look like a novice. If one has a fast flying aeroplane, like the Yak 18, and one is required to fly a super-slow roll (more than 15 seconds) downwind, it does not take a giant intellect to realise that if enough airspeed is retained to fly the roll, the aircraft is going to go out of the box; and indeed some sequences are specifically designed to reduce the chances of the opposition, especially where it is known that at the time of year of the contest, a strong wind generally prevails.

But the news is not all bad; we can, with a little thought, make the wind work for us. We have already seen some of the basic examples; and now we can add to them. If we can arrange for our spin entries to be into wind, we have a much better chance of achieving an early vertical flightpath. At low altitude, where the wind gradient is strong, if one flies a half reverse Cuban 8 into wind, the "kite" effect of the wind will increase the altitude at the top, and the wind shear at the bottom will increase the airspeed.

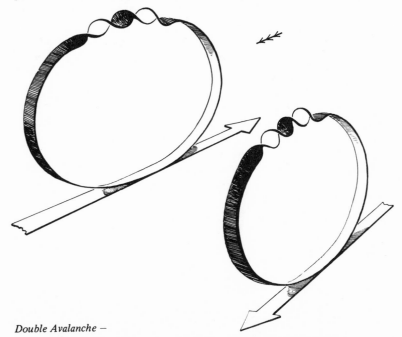

Double Avalanche –

Top drawing – Wind extends flick rolls and impairs shape of overall figure
Bottom drawing – Wind compresses flick rolls and improves shape of overall figure

To prove this statement, do we not lose airspeed in windshear during a landing? If we travel with the wind, the airspeed goes up. A half loop flown into wind, will give more height gain than the same figure flown downwind, assuming the shapes are identical. These are some of the effects of windshear, but let us also consider other wind effects.

If we have a rolling circle, starting into wind, and we have been blown a little downwind beforehand, we can either motor a long way upwind, and lose continuity, or start the circle immediately, and make the turn towards the judges. If we now climb steadily, the speed will fall, and so will our groundspeed downwind halfway round the circle. Because we are coming in towards the judges, the change in elevation makes it look as though we are level, but flying faster. From the halfway mark we start to dive, with the opposite effect, and now our groundspeed is high into wind, which is just want we want, so we finish in the same place, with more airspeed, and no break in continuity.

To consider a looping manoeuvre, if we fly a double avalanche into the wind, the prolonged flicking gives the loop a doughnut shape. Now, if we do this figure downwind, the wind will shorten the flicking line for us and make the figure appear round once more.

In general, it is a good idea to design a sequence that creeps "upwind" at about 10 knots on a still day. This will give us maximum flexibility. The wind is nearly always there; let us use it as an ally, not as a foe.

21 *Advanced sequence construction*

During our initial attempts at sequence construction we were somewhat restricted in that all we did was to assemble all the manoeuvres we could fly in a reasonable order, and then to see if we could get'through it without losing height, direction or both.

These early attempts were aligned, hopefully, with a ground feature, but if we were still aligned at the end of the sequence, it was more a matter of luck than anything else; certainly we were not at that time trying to stay over one spot.

As we progress, and add to our repertoire, we also become more proficient at holding position, until the time comes when we can fly over the airfield at heights down to 1,000 feet. Our basic sequences, with the odd new figure, will still suffice at this stage, where the main problem is still how to keep the aeroplane over the airfield, even in a very light wind. There seems to be so much to try and remember.

With the first basic competition in sight, the problem confronting us is more "what can I put in" rather than "what shall I leave out", and this is where the difference lies between basic and advanced aerobatics.

In an advanced competition one has to consider several points before starting to design the sequence. First, the rules must be understood thoroughly, or one finishes up in one's hotel room at 3 a.m. on the day of the contest, struggling to redesign one's sequence; and that is no way to prepare oneself! If the rules are simple, and one is being marked only for accuracy, and positioning, there is no need to produce exotic manoeuvres; in fact one is throwing away one's chances by doing so.

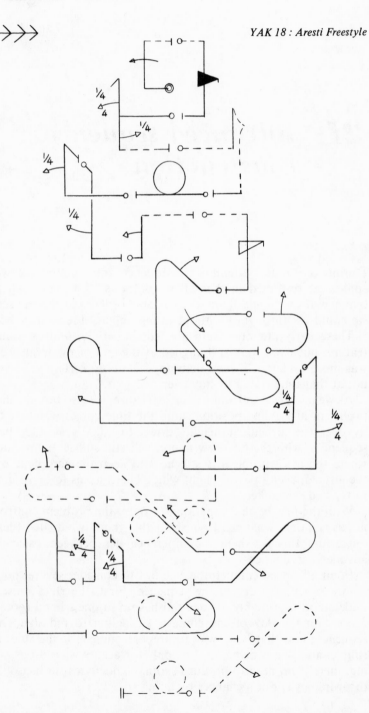

YAK 18 : Aresti Freestyle

Try and arrange for each figure to have a K value of about the average for each figure of the sequence, and use the maximum permitted number of figures; this will give the best chances of a high score.

The general rule is still to have every other figure a turnround manoeuvre, but because of the penalties of going out of the box, sometimes the central figure is omitted, and we go straight from one turnround manoeuvre to another. In the early stages, the thought of devising so many turnround figures would have been demoralising, but here is where a thorough knowledge of the Aresti system will pay off.

Usually the rules state that the first repetition of a figure will score 50 per cent of the original K, the second repetition 25 per cent, and the third and subsequent, zero. Although we can use this method, we can no longer maintain our ideal average score per figure, so this is not a good system, except in emergency. Let us consider a typical Yak 18 sequence for 650 total K. The Soviet pilots are past masters at this freestyle Aresti sequence, and their continuing successes in competition work proves not only their high standard of flying, but also the amount of preparation and thinking on the ground, and this is where the contests are really won or lost. The sequence appears to be full of quarter rolls, but a close inspection will reveal that they are all different! Agreed, the sequence looks boring, but we are after points here, since the real spectacle comes in the non-Aresti freestyle sequence later in the contest. All difficult manoeuvres are avoided; safety first is the motto. Note that only a quarter of the rolling circle is flown; with no comparison of segments we must get a high score. The remainder of the mandatory circle is an ordinary steep turn! One needs to be a world class pilot to appreciate the clever design of this sequence.

As a comparison, though it was designed under different rules, requiring a more adventurous approach, I include my own 700 K freestyle, flown in a Zlin 526F, which gained 4th place in the World Championship in 1970. Note how speed is traded for height, and vice versa, and how pairs of manoeuvres are grouped between turnround figures. As a result of this, every inch of the box was required to accommodate the sequence. This particular sequence was designed to have good flow and a graceful appearance. Because even the Zlin loses height, I included two upward looping figures into rolling circles, which allowed a height gain and a build up of energy.

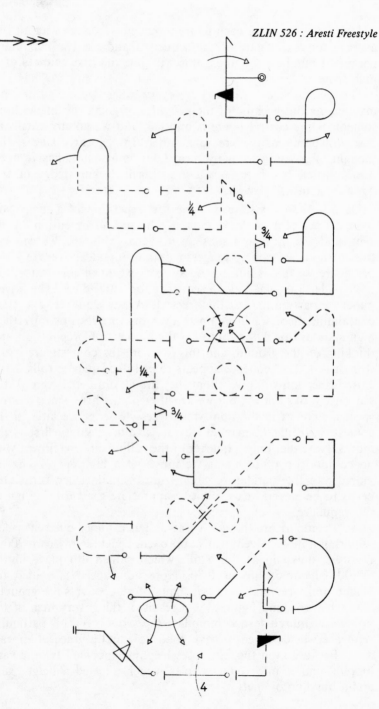

Style plays an important part in a sequence, and I tend to fly large, and hopefully dramatic, manoeuvres. A disadvantage of this system is that it brings one perilously near the edges of the "box". The final line in my sequence includes a vertical roll, tailslide, and inverted spin, starting and finishing on the bottom height limit of 100 metres. No margin for error, but it will result in a higher score than if it were higher up. The judges, after all, are only human!

Positioning plays a very large part in the scoring of individual figures, whether the rules say so or not. If a judge has to crane his neck and squint into the sun, he is not going to give such a good score as if the manoeuvre were at a comfortable viewing angle. He will not do this intentionally; it can be put down to the irritation factor!

One of the biggest problems of designing a high pointed yet simple sequence is to find a sufficient number of turnround figures, since on the face of it we will run out of them very quickly, especially if we are flying a tight-knit sequence, with no central figures. Another look at the Yak 18 sequence will produce the fact that he has no less than sixteen complete turnround figures, all of them different, so obviously they are there, if we only care to look for them.

It is often useful to have several manoeuvres on the "B" axis, if only to allow us to adjust position in a crosswind. For example, if there is a strong on-judge wind, we will want to start on the far edge of the "box", and let the wind drift us in as we get lower, so that we do not have to "lay off" drift. However, if the wind is really blowing, we might be grateful for a "little box" (which occurs three times in the Russian's sequence) to allow us to adjust lateral position. These "little boxes" can be flown either towards, or away from, the judge, as required by the competitor.

Ideally the aircraft should work closer to the judges as it gets lower, to maintain a good viewing angle, and at the same time the amount of the "A" axis covered should be reduced, so that the judge is only aware of the quality of the positioning when he has to give it a mark. If he has not had to think about it during the performance, the positioning must have been near perfect.

When designing a sequence on paper, one can get a very good idea of the amount of space it is going to need by keeping all the Aresti symbols in proportion. If one finds oneself getting near the edge of the card, one can be sure that on the day, one will be in danger of going out of the "box". We have only to compare the

Yak sequence with my Zlin programme to verify the fact that I was operating much closer to the edges of the "box".

The overall shape of the sequence if drawn with all the Aresti figures in proportion will also closely approach the actual shape of the sequence as it will appear in the air. When one studies the sequence card, it should be the same one that is carried in the aeroplane, to avoid confusion. It is always difficult to know where to begin when designing a free sequence. For training purposes one may wish to select a favourite starting and finishing figure, and then place various combinations of pleasing manoeuvres down on paper, after which they may be assembled rather like a jigsaw puzzle. One can easily adjust the required number of points by altering the number of rolls in a rolling circle, or reversing the direction of roll, or by adding rolls to stall turns and tailslides, or by any of hundreds of different methods, while still retaining the basic shape of the sequence.

On the other hand, one can assemble a list of simple figures, mostly turnround, and fly them, as do the Yak pilots.

The rules change over the years, and one must study them carefully. Perhaps the most spectacular Aresti sequences were seen ten years ago when there was no top limit on the K value, only a limit of 25 figures maximum! As an example of this, let us look at Bezàk's sequence designed for a Zlin 226 Akrobat Special, amounting to nearly 900 K! Here we have the full spectrum of aerobatic flying at its best; no restrained, cautious flying here.

Difficult, complex, and fast moving it held both spectators and judges enthralled. It is not necessary to rely entirely on a powerful and agile aeroplane to do well, because in the same competition D'Orgeix of France flew a Stampe into tenth place with a clever sequence, which is obviously conserving precious altitude with practically every manoeuvre.

The real answer in sequence design is to thoroughly know one's aircraft, its strong points and its failings, and to exploit the former and avoid the latter. It is even more important to know one's own capabilities, because one can, given a reasonable level of skill, make even a low powered machine perform quite well, whereas merely acquiring the best aerobatic aeroplane in the world will not ensure success. One *can* make a silk purse out of a sow's ear, but it does take time!

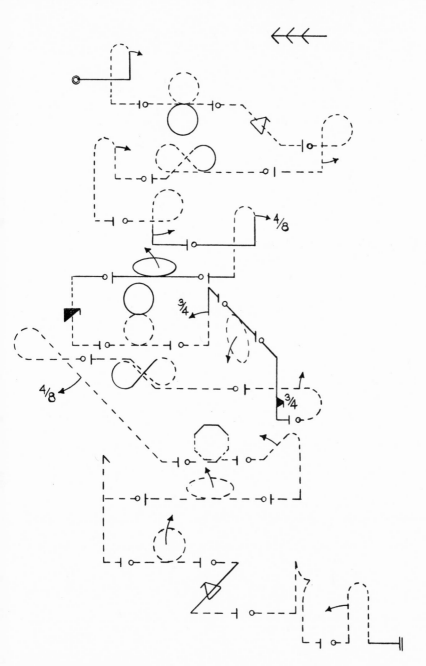

ZLIN 226 : *Aresti Freestyle*

One should therefore begin by planning a sequence which is within the capabilities of both pilot and aircraft. Since we will have to operate inside the "box", design the sequence so that it looks right on the card. Try to arrange for it to "creep" into wind at an average wind speed of 10 knots, and try to play speed against height to preserve the energy content of the aeroplane. One can always learn from other pilot's successes – and failures!

22 *What is a lomcovàk?*

During the 1950s there was a wonderful event called the Lockheed Aerobatic Trophy, which attracted pilots from all over Europe. The contest consisted of an exact five minute period in which one had to extract the maximum from the pilot/aeroplane combination, and where competitors were encouraged to "paint a picture in the sky", as the chief judge put it. Five minutes is not a very long time when it comes to demonstrating everything that one can do (or thinks one can do) in an aerobatic aeroplane, yet the contest was extremely popular, perhaps because the atmosphere was so relaxed.

The first day was devoted to practice flights over the airfield, and we all turned out to watch the Czechs practice in their Zlins. What happened that day left us dazed with disbelief. We saw all the laws of aerodynamics and gravity refuted. We saw aeroplanes flying backwards, sideways, tumbling and rotating about all three axes, at zero airspeed, and still apparently under full control. By our standards, what we were watching was completely impossible! But the culmination of it all came when one Zlin described three consecutive forward somersaults, the plane of each circle being at 45° to the one before it; and all with apparently no forward speed at all. This, we were told, was a lomcovàk.

From that moment on, the Czechs knew no peace. Gone were any ideas we may have had about placings in the contest; all we wanted to know was how they did it, and whether it could be done in any other type of aeroplane, for at that time the club was equipped with Stampes. But it was all very confusing, because everyone we talked to seemed to have a different method of executing the manoeuvre. Not until much later did I realise that there are at least five basic lomcovàks, each with several derivatives. At the outset we concentrated on the type known now as the "big" or "main" lomcovàk, which is initiated from a nearly vertical climb. We struggled through the competition, watched the Czechs dazzle pilots and judges alike, and flew back to our base full of ideas and enthusiasm. Our early attempts at carrying out a lomcovàk were undoubtedly hard on both pilot and aeroplane, because we made the mistake of just applying full control in the appropriate direction and hoping for the best. In fact one has to "play" the controls much as a fisherman plays a fish on the end of his line – give a little, take a little.

My first attempt left me more confused than I had been before I started. I entered the manoeuvre from the inverted and pushed up towards the vertical, using full power, at which point I applied the controls to initiate an inverted flick roll. The world exploded into a juddering, whirling, kaleidoscope of green and blue; something hurtled out of the cockpit, narrowly missing my head in the process. I still have no real idea of what the aeroplane did that day, but when I got it sorted out, the entire "P" compass was missing! We never found it.

This made us realise that if we continued the bull-in-a-china-shop technique something was going to break. So for several years I experimented, proceeding by very slow steps, until I could produce a spectacular, safe, figure with very low *g* forces. But still I could never predict with 100 per cent accuracy where the aeroplane would finish. I always refused to tell people how I entered the manoeuvre, because I still didn't understand fully what was going on, and I knew by this time that there was the very real possibility of badly overstressing the aeroplane. The figure I was flying, though it looked spectacular, was evidently not a real lomcovàk, because once I had initiated it I no longer had any real measure of control, whereas I was certain that the Czechs' manoeuvres were controlled.

Then came the breakthrough, when I had the opportunity to talk to and fly with the ex-world champion, Ladislav Bezàk of Czechoslovakia, who was originally responsible for conceiving the lomcovàk. He explained the more common types to me, and demonstrated them in the air. Initially I used the Stampe, but when I tried some lomcovàks in a Zlin I could see instantly why the Czechs had been able to control this strange figure so precisely. More than that, when the manoeuvre is flown correctly, it is incredibly gentle!

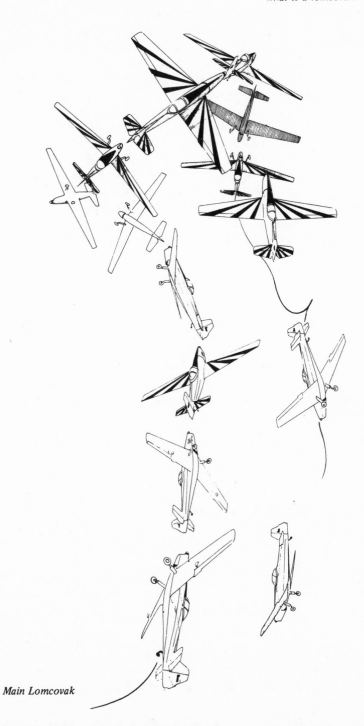

Main Lomcovak

Compared with our earlier efforts, everything seems to happen in slow motion, with the exception of the figure I had been trying to fly for so long, the "main" lomcovàk. This one is a multiple turn figure and I have not found it necessary to change my technique very much: but I have decided that I will only fly it with an aircraft equipped with a wooden propeller, as I feel that the gyroscopic forces involved are too high if a metal propeller is fitted. Also, for the general safety of the aeroplane I feel that these manoeuvres should not be entered at an angle of more than 45° from the vertical climb, otherwise the dissipation of airspeed is not sufficiently high before the rotation builds up, and the chain reaction from this can cause damage to the aeroplane.

All these manoeuvres can be entered from a speed equal to the maximum straight and level speed in a biplane, or 85 per cent of the maximum straight and level speed in a monoplane. However, it should be remembered that most of the so-called aerobatic aeroplanes today are really only semi-aerobatic, and therefore should not be subjected to these manoeuvres.

The "main" lomcovàk is entered from a climb which is slightly over the vertical, the level speed before the climb having been as described above. If the propeller turns anticlockwise as seen from the cockpit, the inverted flick roll is initiated with left rudder, and stick forward and to the right. At this point the flightpath becomes vertical. The yaw and roll resultant then precesses owing to engine/propeller gyroscopic forces, and the aeroplane reaches a state where all the rotation is about the lateral axis in a forwards direction, this axis being vertical with respect to the earth.

At this point one has the option of leaving full power on and continuing the "main" lomcovàk, with the lateral axis itself precessing after the first turn until it is again horizontal; alternatively, one can use the throttle to achieve a "cap" lomcovàk. In the first case, if the entry has been fast in terms of control application, it can produce three complete turns; the last being a forward loop on the spot with nil airspeed. It can also cause damage to the aeroplane, so I personally restrict it to two turns, by entering the figure more gently. One can also finish up in an inadvertent tail-slide, with fully deflected controls.

By leaving full power on, a steady roll around the longitudinal axis of the aeroplane can be maintained: this is not due to the ailerons because airspeed is almost zero. In the case of the "cap" lomcovàk the intention is to make a forward loop of 360° with the lateral axis vertical to the earth; therefore the engine is used

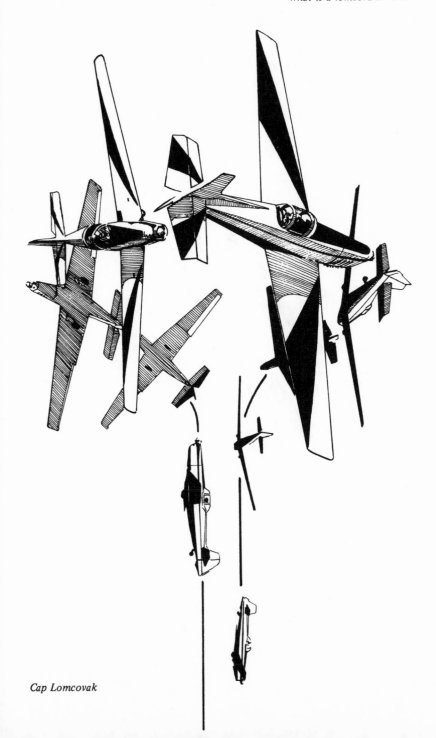

Cap Lomcovak

smoothly as an extra aerodynamic control to prevent any further roll around the "A" axis once the "B" axis is perpendicular. Since the rotational force for the complete manoeuvre comes from the engine, throttling down will slow the pitch rate almost to zero, and this should be reached after one complete rotation.

In our aircraft as described above the right wing will be towards the ground. The stick is pulled fully back and full left rudder is applied: this initiates a sideslip to the right, just enough so that

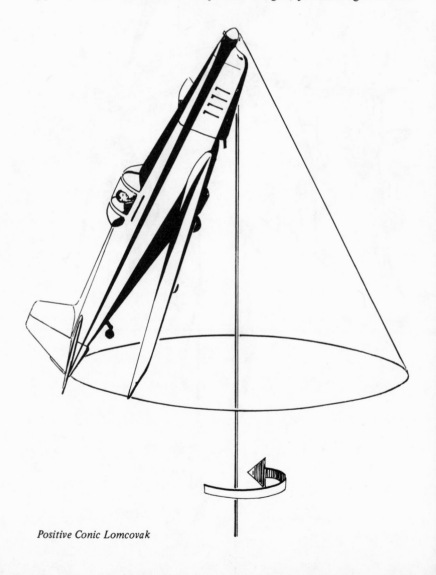

Positive Conic Lomcovak

when the rudder is reversed and power applied, one exits in the same manner as from a stall turn to the right. If this rudder reversal technique is not used, the aeroplane will roll onto its back and sink out of control. The "cap" lomcovàk can also be entered from a climb just short of the vertical, but this time using right rudder.

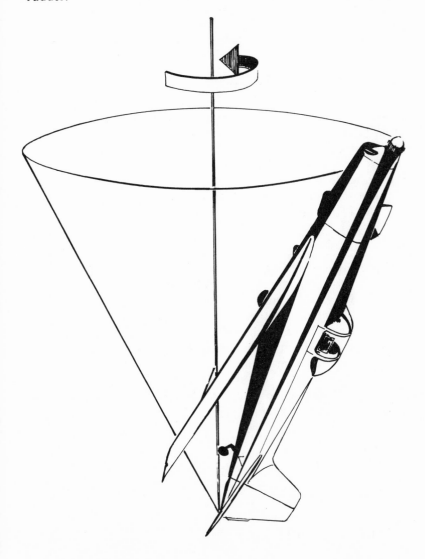

Negative Conic Lomcovak

Of all the lomcovàks, the "conic" lomcovàks are by far the prettiest and cleanest. The positive "conic" is inclined at 15° to the vertical, with the nose of the aircraft acting as the focal point and the tail describing a horizontal 360° circle. The path traced by the fuselage is cone-shaped – hence the name. The negative "conic" is 15° beyond the vertical, and this time the aircraft's tail is the focal point, while the nose describes the circle. The exit from the positive "conic" is a stall turn or tailslide, while the exit from the negative "conic" is by tailsliding or simply pitching over into a vertical dive.

Perhaps the most difficult thing about flying lomcovàks is the need to use the throttle, not as a "go faster" lever, but as an extra aerodynamic control. This is why the "conic" lomcovàks are easier than the others, in that there are only two required positions for the throttle – open or shut. In the case of the positive "conic" the throttle is closed as soon as rotation starts, and is opened to recover, while in the negative "conic" the throttle is left wide open until the moment of recovery, when it is closed. Needless to say, the latter is the more violent.

During these lomcovàks, initiated from a near vertical attitude, there is considerable pilot disorientation. All lomcovàks are flown under negative *g* regardless of the type of entry, so that one is subjected to very high rates of rotation often in three planes simultaneously, while subjected to an inverted loading. This can make it quite difficult to think coherently. Since the pilot is sitting somewhere near the C.G. he is not very far from the centre of rotation, so that after the initial peak of negative *g* he may be in a very low *g* environment during the steady rotation. It is as well to consider what is going on at the extremities of the aeroplane, especially in terms of the gyroscopic forces at the propeller when the engine is at full power.

Another type of lomcovàk which is rather hard on the aero-plane, unless great care is taken, is the lomcovàk from sliding knife flight in a 45° climb. The further the angle from the vertical, the more violent the manoeuvre. This one is started as an inverted climbing flick roll, and progresses to the state of the "main" lomcovàk. It is the only time I ever saw an aeroplane going upwards, backwards! Several Zlins have lost their propellers during this manoeuvre, though it can be done safely, if one is prepared to throttle back.

There is only one variation of the lomcovàk which can be started from anything less than a 45° climb and that is the "tumble", which is entered from inverted horizontal flight, but at a very low airspeed, in fact very near to the inverted stalling speed. Even so, unless one throttles back in the early stages of rotation, the yaw rate accelerates dramatically, and damage usually results.

In this figure, the aircraft quickly goes from an inverted flick roll into a horizontal inverted flat spin, which is fully developed by the end of the first turn, resulting in the aircraft pointing vertically upwards. Since it is still yawing rapidly, the last 180° of rotation is the same as a stall turn, as far as the recovery goes, except that with the stick fully back the ailerons may be used in the outspin mode to augment recovery, but *only* after the accelerometer begins to give a positive reading. If the throttle is not closed after this manoeuvre commences, besides the danger of severe disorientation, and engine damage, there is usually heavy airframe buffet present in some types. The safety of the manoeuvre depends entirely on a low entry speed and an early throttle closure.

The smaller the aeroplane, the wilder and more spectacular will these manoeuvres evidently be. They will also be less controllable and less pretty to watch. The combination of a very small aeroplane with a very large engine will give the most uncomfortable ride imaginable, since the manoeuvre is primarily a gyroscopic one. For the same reason an aeroplane fitted with a metal propeller will probably produce more prolonged rotation than an identical aeroplane fitted with a wooden propeller.

Although the lomcovàk is widely used throughout the world in freestyle flying and in displays, it is not really understood. Pilots talk about "the lomcovàk" as though there were only the single manoeuvre, but as we have seen, the term can cover a wide variety of gyroscopically controlled figures. They do not appear in the Aresti dictionary because they have hitherto not been regarded as properly controlled manoeuvres, except, perhaps in Czechoslovakia, where they define the lomcovàk as "A rapid negative roll executed in that direction towards which the torque of the propeller is helping in rotation."

The real origin of the name lomcovàk comes from the Slovak slang expression for a large, stiff drink. A Czech pilot once likened the sensation to the result of consuming rather too much plum brandy – I can well believe it!

23 *Tailslides and torque rolls*

Really the title is a bit of a misnomer, because the torque roll is actually a rolling tailslide, so it is therefore convenient to look at the two manoeuvres together, in spite of the fact that while every aircraft can tailslide, not all of them can torque roll.

The tailslide is probably one of the most dangerous of all aerobatic manoeuvres, and this is why it is placed towards the end of the syllabus. It is also why, right at the beginning, we learned the recovery from the vertical, so as to avoid the inadvertent tailslide.

Aeroplanes were never designed to fly backwards, and the result of doing this places very high loads on the control surfaces and linkage. We know from experience how savagely a strong wind can slam across the controls of a parked aeroplane, and this may give us an idea of what to expect if we allow the controls to deflect in a tailslide. It will sometimes take all our strength to prevent the controls from banging against the stops: if we fail to hold them central we can expect damage in some form. Sometimes it will be stretched control cables, or maybe, and this is very common, a rudder damaged through coming into contact with the elevator. Usually, if you try to make them touch when you are on the ground it cannot be done, so this is another example of the forces at work.

The perfect tailslide is usually accepted as being over a distance equal to two fuselage lengths, and this is where small aircraft like the Pitts would seem to have the advantage. However, one length is generally considered acceptable, in the interests of safety, and at the same time there should be no unwanted yaw or roll to spoil

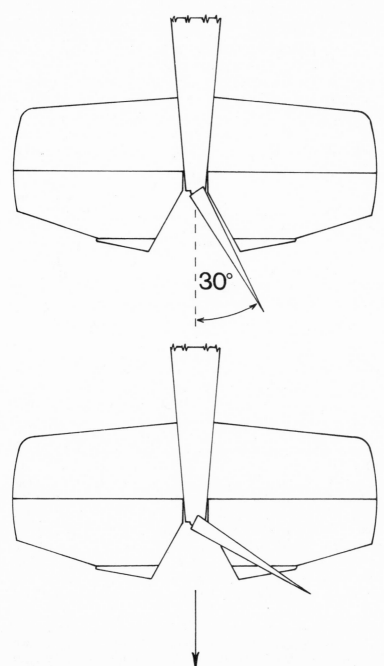

Typical full rudder deflection, and possible consequence of allowing rudder to deflect in tailslide

the manoeuvre. The bigger the aeroplane, the less it will be affected by engine torque with the attendant roll problems, so perhaps the Pitts does not have the advantage after all; and in fact, we will find out that Pitts' pilots tend to avoid tailslides wherever possible, because of this. But as with all manoeuvres, it can be done cleanly, if you know your aeroplane!

The best tailslides are usually the result of having placed the aircraft exactly vertical, but this too brings its problems. If the attitude is precisely vertical, and we do nothing about it, the aircraft might topple forwards or backwards, and if it goes the wrong way we will be scored zero. Also, we have seen what engine effects can do, so it follows that the throttle must be fully closed when the aircraft is stationary, otherwise we will have a sufficient tendency towards torque rolling to spoil the manoeuvre. It also means that we stand a risk of stopping the propeller!

Although there are many different tailslide combinations, with various rolls, flicks and spins, there are really only eight basic tailslide figures, and if we further reduce this by ignoring entry and exit combinations, we can bring the manoeuvre to the simplest possible level by considering the slide with the stick back (falling forwards) and the slide with the stick forward (falling backwards). Sometimes called "canopy up" and "canopy down" tailslides respectively, if we refer to them by the stick position it will help us to avoid mistakes when flying them.

The basic form of the stick back tailslide requires a vertical climb, a two length straight slide, falling forwards into a vertical dive.

In still air, we really will have to achieve the vertical climb, using full power initially. The point at which one throttles back will depend entirely on the aircraft used: one can maintain power on the Zlin until just before appreciable left rudder would be required to keep straight, whereupon the throttle is fully closed, and then opened one inch. This last action will not produce anything immediately, but will ensure that the engine will be available when required later! As the Zlin starts to slide, we apply full power, because we know there is going to be a delay in pickup, and in fact the power will not arrive until we are in the vertical dive. If we did not adopt this system we would have long seconds with no power.

With the Pitts one must throttle fully back as soon as the vertical is achieved, to give the colossal inertia in the propeller time to dissipate, otherwise we will start to torque roll. The Pitts

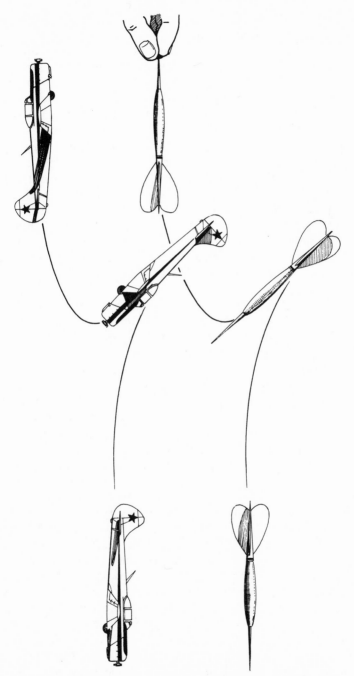

An Aeroplane naturally tends to fall into a dive from any unnatural attitude

will still coast upwards quite a surprising distance before it starts backwards!

Having achieved an exact vertical, since we do not wish to take any chances, when we near the top of the climb, we ease forward on the stick just enough to tip the aircraft a degree or so forward from the vertical, all the while looking at the wingtips to make sure they are exactly level. In the latter stages it is no good looking at the ASI, because there will be nothing to see. The precise moment when one starts to slide is hard to define at first, and the best way of determining it is to listen for the change of slipstream note which heralds the direction reversal. This is the moment one has been waiting for! The stick is brought backwards an inch or two (hence the title) and then everything is held hard: both hands on the stick, elbows in, feet braced, and wait. There is often a lot of control snatching and tramping, but if we did everything right we will get a controlled slide. One can correct an incipient yaw by applying rudder in the *same* direction, but this is taking a bit of a chance. Our elevator position ensures we will drop forward, but when it happens, the rapidity with which the nose goes down is quite startling at first. Try dropping a throwing dart point up, and you will get a good idea of what happens when a tailslide reverses direction! As the machine drops through the horizon, pull the stick fully back to stop the pendulum effects. In fact the nose will still swing through the vertical a little, but it should be placed in the vertical dive as quickly as possible without misusing the aeroplane. From here on we have a standard recovery from the dive.

If we allowed a little yaw to develop at the top of the manoeuvre, and the aircraft starts to slide out sideways one might as well heave a sigh of despondency and accept the inevitable zero from the judges!

Care should be taken not to apply power too early in the dive with an aircraft such as the Pitts, with its very high power to weight ratio, or one may achieve a diving torque roll, which even full opposite aileron may not be able to prevent initially.

The wind can materially help or hinder the execution of a tailslide, since, if one has pulled up into wind for a stick back tailslide, the fact that the aircraft has to be tipped forward anyway to compensate for wind drift, ensures that the attitude at the top is correct for the slide. In this case, we may not even have to pull the stick back, as merely holding the controls firmly in neutral will produce a slide, which, if the aircraft is not tilted sideways at the apex of the manoeuvre, will fall forwards as required.

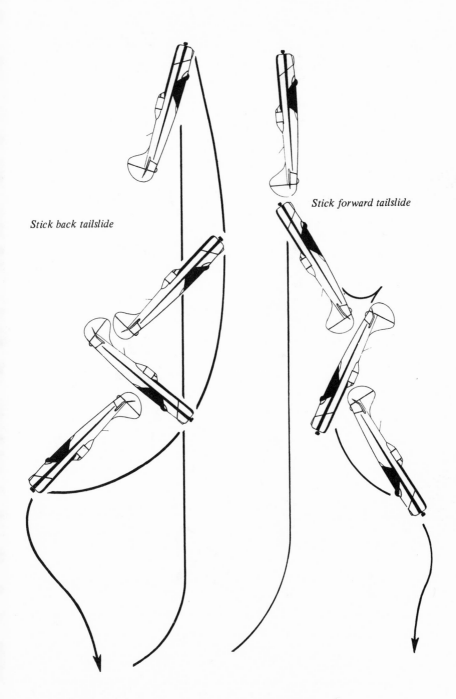

Stick back tailslide

Stick forward tailslide

The stick-back talislide is made easier by flying it into wind

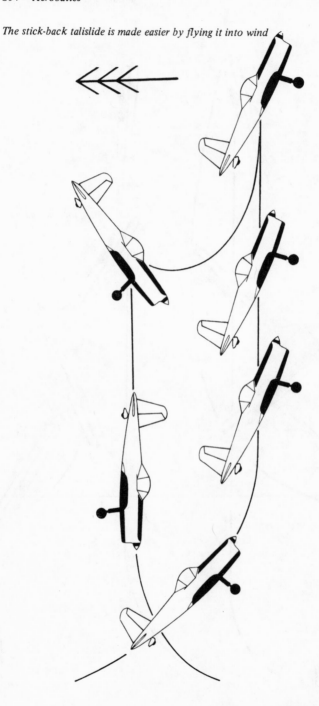

However, if one pulls up downwind, the aircraft must be held *over* the vertical in order to track correctly, and the point where it has to be tipped forward prior to the slide must be chosen very carefully, if one is not to draw an "S" shape in the sky.

At the other end of the scale, if it is not tipped forward far enough, or soon enough, the results may be embarrassing as the machine may fall backwards, which will result in a score of zero. It was this very mistake which deprived the Russian pilot who was defending his World Championship title of his chances of retaining it. He was trying just that little bit too hard for a perfect manoeuvre, and he failed only by a hair's breadth, which produced a groan of sympathy from the other pilots, so near had he been to perfection.

The stick forward tailslide is flown under exactly the same principles as we have just seen, except of course that at the last moment the aircraft has to be tipped backwards a little, and the stick held slightly forward at the moment of sliding.

There is a very powerful tendency for the aircraft to swing through in a pendulum motion, and this is especially true of the stick forward tailslide, so that the elevator, and sometimes the throttle as well, on larger aeroplanes, must be used to control this.

This phenomenon has sometimes been used to good effect where, on the follow-through from a stick forward tailslide, the stick has been pulled fully back with the application of full power, and the aircraft swings through until it actually reaches the horizontal flight position! If full rudder and outspin aileron are then applied, one can immediately enter a flat spin, and this combination is often used by the Russians, since the big Yak 18 flies the figures easily.

Sometimes, the most dramatic manoeuvres are quite simple to fly, and in theory at least, the torque roll is just such a manoeuvre. The big secret is to make sure that the figure is started in an absolutely true vertical climb, and although this sounds simple, it is not easy to achieve in practice: if a torque roll doesn't come off, one can be fairly sure that the initiating roll was not vertical.

The entry is made at high airspeed for best dramatic effect, and in the case of the Pitts, left aileron is used, so that the engine torque helps the roll; however the roll should be entered smoothly, never sharply, as the sudden application of aileron can cause a departure from the vertical. The roll is maintained until the forward speed is zero, and now the torque is the only force which is keeping the aeroplane rolling. Just before it starts to slide backwards, full right aileron is applied; if this movement is not perfect, the aircraft will drop sideways. This aileron reversal technique is only necessary on the Pitts S2A; on the smaller Pitts SI.S, any harsh movement will disturb the sensitive vertical attitude, so on this aeroplane the ailerons are not reversed. The very powerful torque force will give an adequate roll rate against the ailerons.

In the case of the Pitts S2A, with the aircraft sliding backwards, the ailerons (now reversed), will continue to accelerate the left roll, and the result is a rolling tailslide. The idea is to complete an exact number of turns, and then stop the roll (by centralising the ailerons and closing the throttle), and then making the aircraft slide straight for one fuselage length before selecting which way it will topple out, by moving the elevator the opposite way, as in the basic tailslide. It is possible to "steer" a torque roll, by literally "flying" the aeroplane backwards, but this is so unnatural, that, coupled with the extreme aircraft instability in reverse flight, it is not really a practical proposition!

The Torque Roll

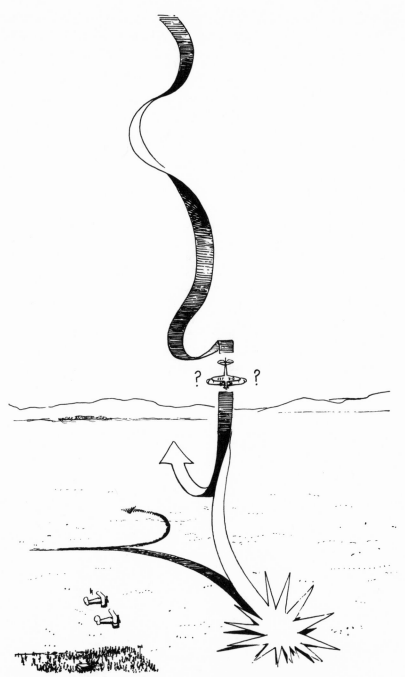

The most useless commodity in aerobatics is the amount of sky above you!

The torque roll is not an Aresti manoeuvre, which is perhaps a good thing, as otherwise it might appear in a compulsory programme, and it is, at the best of times, a somewhat hit and miss affair. It also puts more strain on the aeroplane than almost any other manoeuvre.

It is used to best effect at low altitude, and as such has more of a place at an airshow, rather than a competition. However, it has been used to good effect at a World Championship, in the non-Aresti freestyle sequence, and helped the present world champion to achieve his position, using a Pitts SI.S.

If anything goes amiss with a torque roll at very low altitude, it does not give the pilot much time to sort it out, bearing in mind that he cannot see the ground beneath him when he is in the manoeuvre. Agreed that this also applies to a tailslide, but at least one can take stock of the situation at the apex of a tailslide, and decide whether to carry on or to abandon. In the torque roll, the exact height of the exit cannot be forecast with any real degree of accuracy, and neither can the precise exit line be selected beforehand. Most pilots rely on some degree of roll or spin after the aircraft has dropped through, to realign themselves, and this inevitably can only be done at the expense of more altitude.

It is worth considering that the most useless thing in aerobatics is the amount of sky above you!

24   *Knife flight and bridges*

For years efforts have been made to permit aeroplanes to fly inverted as efficiently as they do normally, but it is typical of man's natural curiosity and sense of exploration that no sooner has this been reasonably well achieved than he turns his attention to other areas.

Knife flight in its basic form has been around for a long time, and has been taught at training schools for many years; except that they called it sideslipping, and used it to lose altitude on the landing approach. It has also been adapted to airshow flying, where a long, low, sideslipping run never fails to impress. Still at the airshow, how many times have we seen an exhibition of crazy flying, which could not have been as effective without our old friend the sideslip.

Knife flight is, then, only a sideslip carried to the extreme of using 90° of bank. In a normal sideslip, a certain amount of wing lift is used, but in the true knife edge condition, the wings are not used at all, except as a large vertical fin, with multiple rudders, i.e. the ailerons! All the control really comes from the elevators and rudder, the former being used to maintain direction, and the latter providing the necessary force to incline the nose to an angle where level flight can be achieved. The lift comes from two sources; first the fuselage, lying on its side, forms a rather inefficient wing of sorts, and secondly, the inclined thrust vector of the powerful engine gives a component of lift, as well as providing enough thrust to overcome the colossal drag. Because the whole machine lacks efficiency, knife flight is usually not a protracted affair, although the Pitts, which excels in knife flight, can fly in level knife flight for about a mile, before drag and gravity take over!

A further complication arises in that whereas engines are designed to operate under positive, negative and sometimes even zero *g*, any substantial lateral force can cause the oil to move away from the pickup point which will result in oil starvation. For this reason some aircraft take more kindly to knife edge flight in one particular direction, as evidenced by the higher oil pressure during the manoeuvre. During all knife flight the oil pressure should be carefully monitored.

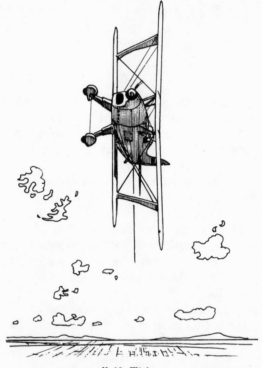

Knife Flight

Now, with the basic principles added to a little practice, what a wealth of diversity opens before us, for the knife edge is not restricted to level flight, but can be used in its own right in any plane, or combined with existing manoeuvres. These figures, employing knife flight, are amongst the prettiest aerobatic manoeuvres to be seen, and they have the advantage of not imposing any severe strain on the aeroplane, as long as we remember our old friend Va, the maximum speed for full control application. We also remember that in aerobatics we never get something for nothing, so where is the catch?

The answer is simply drag, with its attendant loss of energy and height. An aeroplane in flight is charged with energy, which we dissipate in a controlled manner throughout the sequence, aiming to finish with all of it expended. We can prepare the machine by accelerating in level flight at full power before diving for speed to start, thus building up a good store of potential and kinetic energy.

During the sequence we trade these two forms of energy against each other; in effect, playing yo-yo's. Also we have periods of acceleration, at our best operating speed range, to "re-charge" the aircraft. The two most common forms of drag which offset this formidable input of energy are "profile" (high speed needed to roll vertically), and "induced" (the result of high *g* and flick rolls). Now, in the knife edge, we have another form of profile drag due to sideslip, so that if we include many knife flight man-oeuvres, we can expect to lose height quickly. We can, however, afford a few performance losses in exchange for some attractive and impressive figures. A simple form of this type, which does not lose too much energy, is the knife edge loop, which consists of a normal first quarter loop, followed by a fast quarter roll, and an immediate application of rudder to yaw the aeroplane around the top of the loop into the vertical dive. Another quarter roll back into the normal looping plane, and the manoeuvre is completed normally.

The only precautions to take are to ensure that the aircraft is pulled slightly beyond the vertical attitude in the first quarter, to ensure that the flight path is no less than vertical, otherwise we will finish up with the same situation that we saw with the basic stall turn, where the aircraft would not go right if it was already yawed left, and vice versa. Also the manoeuvre should be started into wind, because wind plays a very important part in knife edge figures; indeed it can make all the difference between a good knife edge manoeuvre and an apparently badly executed stall turn.

It is worth looking at the difference between knife edge loops and stall turns with quarter rolls up and down; and this difference (say in still air) is primarily concerned with airspeed. In the case of the stall turn, the airspeed is close to zero, while in the knife edge loop, the manoeuvre relies on a relatively high speed to give it shape.

On the exit from the knife edge loop, we will find that we need to actually yaw the aircraft through the vertical dive position in order to track vertically prior to the quarter roll downwards. This will probably be beyond the rudder power of the aeroplane, even with full power to help it, so we will again have to compromise by rolling early and injecting a bit of surreptitious elevator to make the transition look correct!

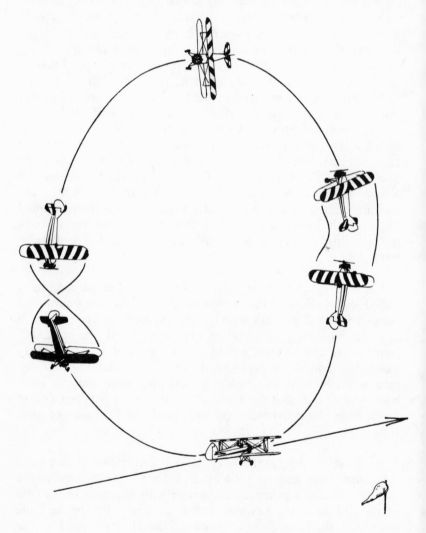

(Bottom) Knife-edge Loop

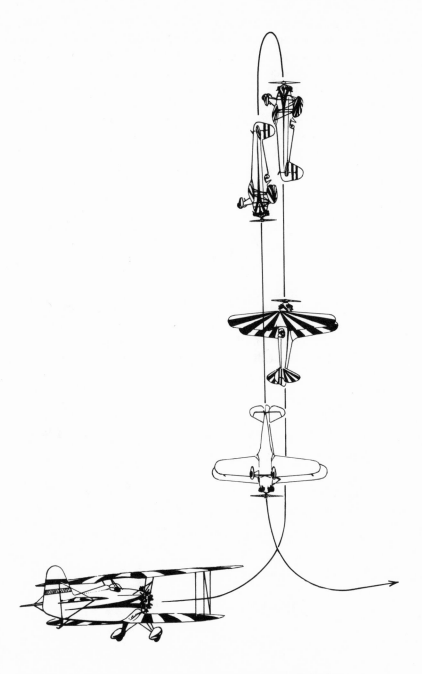

Quarter vertical roll – stall turn – quarter vertical roll out

One of the keys to success in aerobatics is to select all the factors which are working against us, and try to utilise them in our favour, and one of these factors is the wind. We have just seen some of the problem areas due to wind, so let us try aonther knife flight figure with the wind working with us. Such a figure can also be made into a change of direction through 90°. Let us begin on the "A" axis, into wind. Pull up to 45°, and roll through 90°, then hold knife flight in a 45° climb. As the speed falls, the nose will start to drop, but this doesn't matter, as the wind will, at the same time, be trying to steepen the flight path: if we get it right, they will cancel out. At the top, we reverse rudder, and yaw the aircraft rapidly into the vertical, where, because of the large rudder application it will sideslip into wind, and this should result not only in a vertical attitude, but also a vertical flight path, from which we can recover on the "B" axis. In any such knife edge the top of the aeroplane should be presented towards the judges for maximum interest, and in this case it will result in the aircraft running in towards the judges. We can then use another knife edge figure to get back into the "A" axis, merely by flying a half loop and quarter roll, holding it in knife flight for a second, before ruddering down into a pullout on the "A" axis. Of course we will be sideslipping so that our flight path will not be vertical; but this will

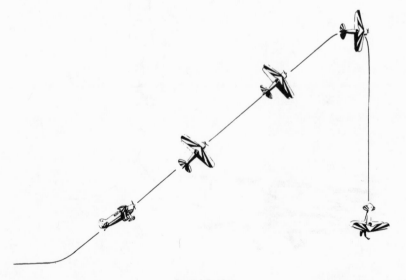

Partial Bridge

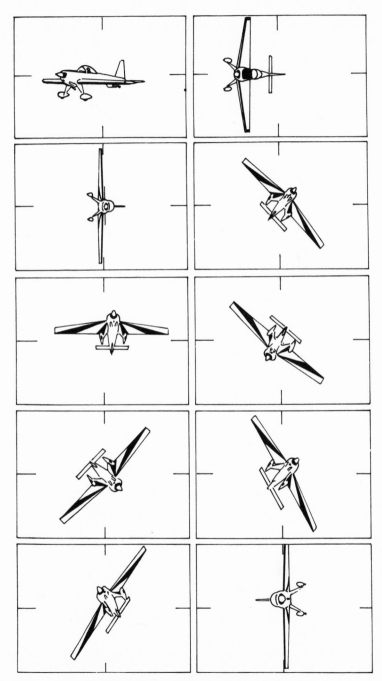

1½ Flick Rolls from knife-edge flight – Judges view

be a sideslip away from the judges and therefore ought not to be detected. We can also use knife flight as a jumping off point for other manoeuvres, for example, the lomcovàk from 45° climbing knife edge.

A very common series of figures are the flick rolls from knife flight and back into knife flight. One of the specialities of the Jungmann with the 180 hp engine is to fly from one end of the "box" to the other, demonstrating a series of inside and outside multiple flick rolls in a staccato dizzy run, pausing in erect, inverted and knife flight only for a split second.

A favourite finishing manoeuvre of the Yak 18 is a one-and-a-half turn inverted flick roll from knife edge flight, stopping with absolute precision in knife edge in the opposite sense. The outside flick roll being rather a Yak speciality this figure is conducted on the 100 metre baseline. I use virtually the same manoeuvre in the Pitts Special, except that I adopt a one-and-a-half turn inside flick roll from knife edge and I fly it straight at the judges on the "B" axis, as the grand finale!

The Bridge

These flicks from knife edge are much faster than normal flicks: they have to be, or the whole manoeuvre jumps sideways, and of course if one is pointing straight at the judges it can be clearly seen. Since the figure will always "translate" to the side to some extent, I start the manoeuvre with the nose 5° to the right of the judges, as I see them. A fast roll to the left into knife, pause, and then stick back and right rudder for the flick. As the figure starts, the aeroplane jumps left and alters heading, so that as I recover, the nose is exactly aligned with the chief judge's table!

The "bridge" is a variant of knife flight, and as with so many new figures, came from Czechoslovakia. Here one pulls up to the vertical and rudders slowly and easily across the top of a yawed loop, until the vertical dive is achieved, followed by a pullout. It can be likened to a stall turn except that by definition the exit flight path must be at least two spans clear of the entry path. It looks what it is; a bridge, and is best seen on the "B" axis, on the far side of the box. Aeroplanes which perform well in knife flight are very good in rolling circles and loops, indeed, with the Pitts one can rudder into a steep climb after a knife edge level run. It will only be a matter of time before an aircraft is designed which can fly a complete loop in knife edge!

25   *Aerobatics unlimited*

When aerobatics really began to get under way again during the post-war years, the Lockheed Aerobatic Trophy was devised. This drew pilots from all over the world, among them Aresti; for this was the Mecca of aerobatic flying, before the present series of World Championship events were held. The rules were quite simple: a Very pistol was fired, and each pilot then had exactly five minutes to show what he could do with his aeroplane before another Very marked the end of his alloted time. The judges required to see a "picture painted in the sky", so that a clever and skilful pilot, even with an underpowered aeroplane, could still win. It was a wide open contest, and we could fly any manoeuvre we could think of or invent, and indeed, most of us did! A certain amount of "ad-libbing" went on when things got a bit out of hand and the stopwatch showed the end of the five minute period approaching, but such was the skill and improvisation of the pilots that the change of sequence was often undetected, even by the judges.

Although one is still not required to submit one's sequence to the judges beforehand, it is a very good idea to have such a sequence well prepared and practiced, because it is quite easy to improvise when there is no time limit, but another story entirely, with the seconds running out!

At present, the World Championship requires a four minute sequence, while the British National Championship requires five minutes, as did the Lockheed. This is a very different story to constructing an Aresti sequence from the rules and dictionary. Here one does not think "what is the easiest sequence I can compose within the rules?" Rather it is "what is the most spectacular sequence I can think of, which I can still fly?"

Also, the other aeroplanes in the competition must be taken into account. It is no good entering at high speed in a Stampe if one is up against Zlins, or Yaks, or Akrostars; and if one is in a Zlin, there is not much point in entering at low speed, because the impact of the aeroplane is wasted. In this type of competition the entry and exit are very important, and many a contest has been won by the last few figures alone. One is going to have to fly some of the sequence on the "B" axis to get a good score, and I find it best to ignore the basic "box", but to merely centre the performance on the judges.

Wind is of crucial importance: the sequence must last for the precise time whether the wind is calm or blowing at 25 knots or more, since no wind limits are laid down in the British contest. This means that those manoeuvres which are downwind must be accelerated, while those into wind slowed down, and this must be done smoothly, so as not to lose general flow.

It is a bit like an ice-ballet, but on a moving rink! One has four dimensions to work in, and one is marked on accuracy, originality, scope, presentation, positioning, harmony, rhythm and variety, for the overall sequence; and accuracy includes timing to within one second. I personally train to within half a second; judges have been known to be slow on the stopwatch!

Before constructing a sequence, one should ask oneself "if I were a judge, what would I want to see?" Since the judges probably don't know anyway, this is a difficult one. A study of sequences, styles and marks will not help you win this competition but will give you a very good idea of how to go about next year's competition.

One should consider the capabilities of all the aeroplanes one knows are going to enter, and ask oneself, "what does my aircraft do best", and "what can I do best." If you are flying a Zlin don't overdo the flick rolls if you are up against a Pitts or a Jungmeister; nothing will flick better than them! Instead go for clean vertical rolls, and graceful easy flying; you could win on style. Everybody has a natural and different style which should be allowed to come out, so don't try to copy anybody else's; it probably won't work for you. Just concentrate on flying accurately and smoothly, and one day style will arrive!

When starting to design an "unlimited" free-style sequence, I write down the manoeuvres I like to fly, and add to this list until I have a complete spectrum of aerobatic figures. By this time I usually have too many, so I either have to disregard some, or turn them into composite manoeuvres so that I have a bit of everything. There is, however, a danger here, in that one can compose a sequence full of sound and action which will result in an explosion of colour instead of that magic "picture in the sky".

Sometimes, in a simple machine, there can be real beauty in a simple sequence flown in a leisurely manner. As a rough guide, for five minutes, one will need 15 figures in a Stampe against 17 in a Zlin and 19 in a Pitts, and this is an indication also of the probable tempo of the sequence. These are of course, nearly all composite figures, some of them with up to five elements. Once the figures have been selected, they should be assembled like a jigsaw, but starting somewhere in the middle, so that we can have interesting combinations on lines, which can themselves be transposed to any part of the sequence, or turned around as required. By now one should have a very clear idea of the starting and finishing manoeuvres, but be careful not ot use manoeuvres which are being flown by other pilots! There is an unwritten rule that these figures are "copyright" and as such shall not be stolen!

Having arrived at the sequence proper, one must then fly it over the area, to see how it looks for positioning, and this should ideally be done in calm conditions as well as a wind. If this is satisfactory, time the whole sequence from beginning to end and see how near you are to the correct time. Perhaps it will be necessary to add or subtract a figure to get the time right, but remember not to rush the sequence: it is better to drop a manoeuvre and slow down a little. As the sequence assumes its final form, time checkpoints should be inserted: every 30 seconds at first, and tightening up as the sequence progresses so that in the last two minutes we know to the second where we should be.

Let us take a look at some typical sequences, starting with the four minute free style sequence of the current World Champion, flying a Pitts SI-S. His starting height is only 500 feet, but he is going very fast indeed, as we can see by his opening manoeuvre, which is a vertical roll right followed by a four point vertical roll left and stall turn, with one outside and one inside flick roll on the exit diving line. The next figure is a corruption of the outside avalanche, in which he includes an extra inside flick roll. Notice the thought which has gone into producing unusual manoeuvres, culminating in the torque roll and triple horizontal flick roll.

Pitts Special : 4 minute Freestyle

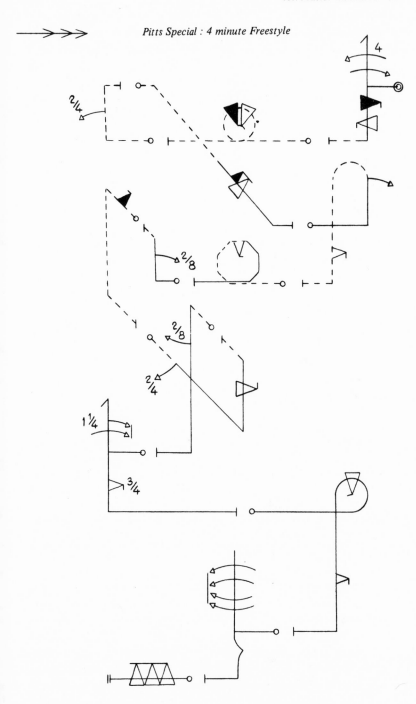

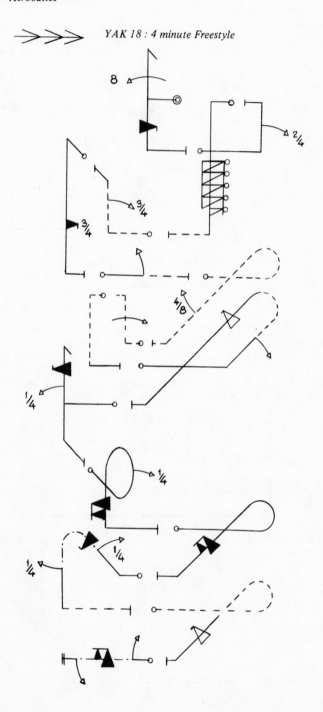

YAK 18 : 4 minute Freestyle

A major feature of this sequence is the large number of flick rolls in which positive flicks predominate, and we would not be surprised, on seeing this sequence on paper, to learn that it was designed for a Pitts. Now to a completely different aeroplane: the Yak 18.

Although we saw that the Pitts had a tremendous vertical performance, it really had very little in the way of vertical rolls in the sequence. The Yak, on the other hand, also has an excellent vertical rolling performance, but more important, it has grace and beauty in flight, and the Soviet pilots exploit this to the maximum. The Yak, then, starts with a vertical eight point roll, which consumes the entire vertical extent of the "box". A stall turn, followed by a one turn negative flick roll on the dive, is quite sufficient in this big aeroplane to look impressive, but now the Yak needs speed! This is an aeroplane that really needs to use the yo-yo technique, and the second figure is designed to have the maximum gain of height, ready for No. 3, which is a flat spin. Though it spins well enough, the Yak does not like inside flick rolls, and we see only two of these in the sequence, both on a 45° descending line: very easy. The inverted flick roll, however, is rather a speciality of the Yak, and we have these in every plane possible, in contrast to the Pitts, where they are not so popular.

This Yak sequence is beautifully shaped so that as it comes lower it uses less and less of the "A" axis, and also comes in close to the judges. Right at the end we have a lot of inverted flicks and knife edge work, the last figure being the Yak "speciality" of a knife edge negative flick.

Notice how, on these sequences, all the flying is done into or across wind; the only time the aeroplane points downwind is to make one turnround figure to come back into wind again. There is no time to spare so one cannot afford to be blown downwind.

As a comparison, I include my own Pitts free sequence which lasts one minute longer since it was designed for the British National Championship. The emphasis is still on a powerful figure to start with, and I also favour starting on the "B" axis. This is to make sure the judges are paying attention because one can never fail to watch an aeroplane that is approaching in a head on dive! The opening figure is the "totem pole", described earlier, while the second half square loop is merely a height gainer. Into the "A" axis and one manoeuvre is conspicuous by its absence, the tailslide – no chances are being taken. The emphasis is on an ebb and flow of action, like a piece of music,

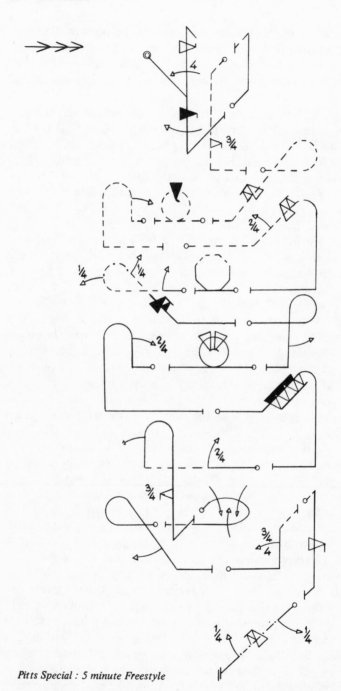

Pitts Special : 5 minute Freestyle

with academic figures interspersed with extravagant exotica such as the "flying saucer" which resembles an upward multi-turn spin.

A horizontal circle is included to add another dimension to the sequence, but because of the time factor I must fly it at double the speed: only possible in a Pitts and with months of training so that it does not look rushed. The grand finale is the knife edge flick straight at the judges on the 100 metre line. This sequence too, follows the general principle of never flying two consecutive manoeuvres downwind in a timed sequence.

I have time and height checks at regular intervals throughout the programme, and as in the Aresti sequences I have designed it to move into wind at 10 knots if I do nothing about it. This means I can control it from flat calm up to 30 knots and still maintain time to within one second, or I can accept 40 knots if I go ten seconds over, but this would only be the case at a display; for I use displays as a dress rehearsal in the knowledge that a carefully prepared sequence of this type is the best from a display point of view.

With a sequence such as this any amount of crosswind can be quite a problem, especially at the start, where the aircraft is at maximum speed on the "B" axis, Since the timing of the sequence starts on the ground, one has to specify the exact time from "brakes off" to starting. This means that the climb has to be planned with the same precision as the sequence, so that the aircraft is at exactly the right point in space twelve seconds before the start, because twelve seconds is the optimum diving time for a Pitts Special. Some correction for small errors in the initial starting position can be made in the second figure, but only at the expense of valuable seconds which will have to be made up later in the sequence. Another opportunity for correction comes during the entry to the rolling circle which must be exactly right otherwise the final figure will be jeopardised.

When one has evolved a really good sequence for one's aeroplane, there is not much point in changing it for change's sake. I have retained the basic concept of my sequence for three years, and have only found it necessary to make fractional changes annually. If I need a four minute sequence I merely delete three figures and modify a fourth, so that I can change sequences with a minimum of re-training.

One day aerobatics may be flown to music, like ice-skating, and if these sequences are always designed to give good flow and rhythm, perhaps we will soon be able to see science and art blended into the ultimate expression of man's aspiration.

26 *Training methods*

It has been said that in flying, there is no substitute for dual instruction, and up to a point, in aerobatics, this is especially true. It is of great importance in the early stages, to receive instruction from a pilot who is not only competent in aerobatics, but can put across his subject with sympathy and understanding, and this will give the student the knowledge and confidence to progress safely. The instructor ought to match the tempo of his teaching to the progress and ability of the student, so that as the level of skill increases, the instructor becomes more demanding, leading the student, but never pushing him. Having introduced the student to the rudiments of flick rolls and inverted flying, it is now time for the instructor to carry on his teaching from the ground, be it airfield or briefing room. A good aerobatic instructor, standing on the tarmac watching his pupil fly, will know what is going on in that cockpit as surely as if he were there. He will see every error, and can usually anticipate mistakes before they occur. This is where other students too, can learn, by listening to what the instructor has to say about the sequence as it progresses. This is quite useful, as it is much better to learn from the mistakes of others where possible. It can be helpful for students to analyse faults, but this should always be done under an instructor's supervision; an error in assessment can compound the mistake. This method teaches students to think clearly on the ground which will then hopefully lead to think constructionally under conditions of stress in the air.

Advanced aerobatics cannot really be taught in the time honoured fashion, i.e. by dual instruction, because the student will be subjected to the instructor's demonstration as well as to the results of his own efforts, and will therefore tire twice as quickly.

Also he will feel that he cannot progress at his own rate, but must force the pace because the instructor is on board. In addition, most aeroplanes either have restrictions on what they are permitted to do at the high weights involved with dual flying, or are simply lacking in performance with two people on board, which doesn't really give the student a chance. Also, some pilots are the owners of single seat aeroplanes, so they cannot possibly use them for dual instruction.

It seems reasonable that if the instructors advice and experience could be carried aloft without the extra weight involved, life would be very much easier. With this in mind, as an experiment, a small radio receiver was built into the aeroplane, with a single channel, powered by a dry cell battery. The whole thing was designed to be compact, and to be able to withstand the stresses involved. The absence of an airborne transmitter was deliberate, since there was no requirement for the student to talk back! The ground unit consisted of a battery operated transmitter and a hand held microphone. This now meant that the instructor remained fresh and could cope with students in different aeroplanes, one after the other, on the same frequency. Also he was able to give all his attention to what the student was doing, since there was no possibility of his taking control. It had the added advantage that the instructor had a much wider field of view and could warn the student of the approach of other machines.

Perhaps the biggest advantage was that it gave the student a tremendous psychological boost in the knowledge that when the aeroplane completed a difficult manoeuvre, he must have actually done it himself, because there was nobody else in the aeroplane! The disadvantages of the system were that the student came to rely on the disembodied voice talking him through the figures, so that when the voice stopped, he reverted to his previous mistakes. In any case, there came a time when the student was thinking so hard about the manoeuvre, that he simply did not hear what was being said to him; he had reached mental saturation. Although there were many definite advantages, especially in the information that could be passed regarding the positioning in the "box", this method was eventually abandoned in favour of a tape recorder, which could be played back by the pilot over and over again, with the sequence card in front of him, until all the points were really rammed home. This repetition of information has proved to be the best way of ensuring that it is in the mind to stay: it is really a primitive form of brainwashing, except that the pilot really does want to learn.

As the sequences became more complex and physically demanding, it became apparent that one could not successfully remain airborne for more than about 20 minutes at a time, otherwise the performance began to deteriorate in an obvious manner, as the learning curve flattened out. After that, it became a waste of time and money. The only thing to do was to land and have a rest. The fact that the tapes had to be played through and thoroughly understood also meant that one had to take a break.

As one becomes more proficient, it is more and more difficult to receive proper critiscism, and eventually the only way to receive such critiscism is from other pilots who are similarly advanced. For safety reasons, it is not wise to train alone, so the "buddy" system has been found to work well.

Even so, there is nothing like being able to see oneself fly, and so experiments were made using cine cameras, and video equipment. The cine film, though interesting, took so long to process that its value as a training aid was lost, so we turned to the video tape. Even here we had a problem, since we wanted to be able to see vertical and 45° angles clearly, and to be able to detect any rotational errors, particularly in upward rolls, and this we could not do because of the narrow angle of the camera. We even tried manufacturing a large multicoloured net which we hung in front of a fixed camera in the hope that it would give us a reference, but it was not a success. What we really needed was a gyro-stabilised camera with cross-hairs at the focal plane, but this was too expensive to consider. We were stuck! Stuck, that is, until somebody, who had been reading about Barnes Wallis, came up with a simple, but brilliant idea. This was quickly acted upon, and the result was a perspex sheet, mounted on an adjustable, and easily transportable frame. This sheet was equipped with a single ring sight, and was so arranged that the vertical and horizontal lines etched on the perspex conformed to the extremities of the "box". Centre lines and maximum and minimum height lines were also included. While this did not show rolling errors in the vertical, it did show all flight paths, and we were astonished to see the powerful effect of wind on our figures. All the operator did was to trace the track of the aeroplane on the sheet with a chinagraph pencil, and there was one's entire sequence in two dimensions! Cheap, simple to operate, it could be used

The Tracking Board

again and again, and is one of our best aids. When used in conjunction with a tape recorder, it is hard to beat. The tracker board,
as we call it, also shows the balance of the sequence about centre,
and as we have arranged for the top and bottom of the board to
make an elevation angle of 75° and 15° respectively with the ring
sight, we can check on lateral position as well as the lower height
limit. If the chinagraph line goes off the top of the board, the
aircraft is too near to overhead the judges, while if the line goes
off the bottom, the aircraft has gone below 100 metres, with the
attendant penalty.

If the weather is bad, and it is impossible to train, we can still
do some useful work. With our model aircraft positioned over
the centre of the lounge carpet, we can "fly" our sequence time
and time again, always trying to visualise what one is going to
see from the cockpit of the real aeroplane. You may see aerobatic
pilots before a competition walking up and down, twisting
their arms and bodies as they go. This is not some primitive
rite, but the concentration of all their attention on the job in hand,
as they "fly" their sequences over an imaginary axis. The programme must be as much a conditioned reflex as possible,
leaving the mind clear to cope with dangers in wind, position,
timing, and all the other variables.

Using models, it is possible to train up to a very high standard
in an incredibly short time, and not only that, the model, if
"flown" realistically, will highlight all the weak points of the
sequences so that these can be eradicated from the start, so
avoiding wasted time and expense.

Naturally it is an advantage to have one's own aeroplane,
but this happy state of affairs is not very common. Most of us
have to share the use of the machine, and we have found with
experience that the maximum number of pilots per aeroplane is
three; any more and the machine is used very hard, and may not
stand up to it, and also no matter how much effort is put in,
nobody seems to get enough flying.

Finally, all serious training should be done at low level over an
airfield, where not only is good criticism available, but there are
safety services on the spot if there is any form of incident: lives
have already been saved by this.

It is no good training at height and then expecting to be able
to come down to 100 metres in the competitions and not be
concerned about it.

A worried, tense pilot, not used to very low altitudes, is not a safe pilot, because he will be tight on the controls, and there will be quite enough problems without adding to them. Serious low level training should not be considered as showing off; in competition work it is excellent insurance: as is plenty of altitude for basic aerobatic students.

27 *Low level aerobatics and display flying*

There is an old aeronautical story which may well have had its foundations in truth many years ago. It has to do with a crew room argument about spinning which resulted in a bet being placed as to who could do the greatest number of turns of a spin from 3,000 feet. The story goes along the lines that the winner staggered shakily from the wreckage, spitting teeth, and demanding his half crown takings!

All very amusing, as a story, but it does underline some of the thinking surrounding air display flying, which can result in unnecessary chances being taken, and has resulted in aerobatics in general being labelled "stunt flying".

To the average member of the public, it is all "stunt flying"; but to the pilots involved, where does one draw the line between "stunting" and aerobatics proper?

The word "stunting" implies a degree of recklessness, a risking of life and limb, and is normally accepted as being done at a very low altitude. It includes "crazy" flying, an act where no normal aerobatic manoeuvres are flown, but it is perhaps true to say that "crazy" flying has a higher accident rate than almost any other form of display flying. This act relies for best impact on its proximity to the ground, in fact some of it is carried out *on* the ground; there is no margin for error, but at the same time, the pilots involved in this kind of accident have a good chance of survival because the altitude is so low that there is not enough room for any great vertical energy to be built up, and this is what usually does the damage.

There is that little devil of showmanship within us all, so that although the act may have been practiced a hundred times quite safely, when it is performed in front of a crowd, a kind of Colosseum attitude takes over, and even cool and experienced pilots sometimes take stupid chances. And this is *not* the time to take any chances, because, with thousands of eyes looking on, one is bound to be a little more tense than one would want to be. The result of this will be a tighter grip of the controls, and one knows that for best co-ordination one should be physically relaxed, so not only will the pilot be pushing his luck but he will not be flying as well as usual. The odds are therefore beginning to mount up, and it is here that the high level of discipline required of the competition aerobatic pilot will stand him in good stead, for he will be accustomed to flying at low level in front of a critical audience.

Since each pilot in conjunction with the requirements of the particular act may have a minimum height ranging from several hundreds of feet down to literally ground level, it is necessary for him to appreciate those aspects of other acts which may require a lower altitude than be himself has planned to use.

Because he hears the gasps of the crowd when a low level high speed fly past is made, it is no reason for him to decide on the spot to reduce the height of his own performance; that way lies disaster. In addition he should remember two points; first, that the crowd have paid good money to be entertained, and not frightened, and secondly, that if he is ultra-low, only the front row of people will be able to see him.

That aside, he will get no vote of thanks from either the display organiser or the authorities if he leaves a smoking heap of wreckage in the middle of the airfield!

There is always a problem when an inexperienced pilot starts flying an airshow routine; he may have come into the business quite suddenly, perhaps because he has acquired an aircraft which is in great demand at displays. He may well feel that he has to put on the same level of display that he sees others doing in similar types; but he should consider that these people have probably been doing it for a very long time; and they will respect him a great deal more if he approaches the difficult art of displaying an aeroplane gradually; after all, if restrictions are eventually imposed because of stupidity, it is their livelihood which will suffer, in many cases.

Each pilot has his own minimum altitude, decided for him by his ability, personality, and temperament, and this will change from day to day, depending on a whole range of variable factors.

Some days he will not feel quite up to it, and that is when the height *must* go up; on other occasions he will be safe at half that height. My own minimum height is about 150 feet for simple rolling manoeuvres, and about 75 feet for a steady straight inverted fly past. These heights are quite low enough for the aeroplane to be clearly seen, and high enough for there to be no concern about the safety of the manoeuvre. Most pilots have a speciality, be it low level flying or anything else. I prefer to leave the really low stuff to others, and to stay higher up and concentrate on really clean flying, because the indication that one has reached one's minimum height for that day is when the standard of the manoeuvres starts to deteriorate.

If one is flying a fully aerobatic aeroplane, then that is exactly what one should let the crowd see, because anyone in any machine can come roaring past at nought feet. If we now consider the judge's requirements for a "picture in the sky", surely this is exactly what we want to put over to the public, remembering that they believe in general that aerobatics and stunt flying are synonymous.

One can really steal the complete show without coming below the lower competition height of 100 metres (328 feet), and at the same time everyone can see comfortably. Ideally one should have a specialised commentator, who can call the manoeuvres a second or so before they happen, and this will really capture the crowd's interest. However, if the commentator is anything less than informed, you will be doing the sport of aerobatics and yourself a favour if, instead, you arrange to have music played over the loudspeaker system. This music need not be synchronised: it is quite surprising how well almost any piece of music will fit, as long as the tempo is more or less right.

Some aeroplanes, like the Spitfire, display themselves, and in this case I try and put on a gentle, rounded display to conform to the superb elliptical lines of the machine. With any vintage types, there must be no hint of harshness or rough or careless flying, because there will be many enthusiasts in the crowd, who have paid their money to enjoy the show, and they will most certainly not enjoy seeing a vintage or veteran machine mishandled or endangered. A point which is often forgotten by many display pilots is that a lot of people want to take photographs, and they will not all have expensive cameras, so there is a good case for flying parallel to the crowd frontage, at less than 100 feet with the aeroplane banked to present its optimum profile. This should be done at a relatively low speed so that some of the youngsters do not finish up with a print which shows a blurred empennage just going off frame.

One of the most important things .to think about is crowd safety. It is unforgiveable for a pilot to endanger the public at a display. To this end, we have seen display regulations and suggestions produced by the authorities and by organisers, and we are reminded of these at the briefing, but we still get crowd infringements. It should be remembered that participation in an air display carries a heavy responsibility and should never be regarded as a jolly, lighthearted affair. By all means enjoy yourselves, but one does not have to be a member of the armed forces to earn the accolade of "professional aviator". I have known pilots with less than 200 hours who were as professional in their outlook as any four-ringed jet captain. It is bad enough to have an accident at an airshow, but it is infinitely worse to crawl semiconscious from the wreckage wondering if one has killed any innocent bystanders. I was once subjected to this devastating experience when an inverted flick roll went wrong in front of 80,000 spectators; but I was one of the few who had adhered to the instructions to stay on the display line: there was nobody in the way when I hit the ground.

One should always keep in the back of one's mind the possibility of a mechanical failure, and the aircraft should be positioned so that there is always an escape route ahead. Even if the engine fails and you are forced to turn downwind into an unsuitable area it is better by far to accept the risk involved rather than to turn towards or over the crowd. At the same time, there is no substitute for common sense; it was said somewhere that "rules are for the obedience of fools and the guidance of wise men". If we take as an example the "safety line" at an air display, this is the line which the aircraft may not cross, and it exists to provide a safety area between it and the crowd frontage. In the case of a hard turn which is aimed to approach closely to this line, and is slightly misjudged, the pilot may have the choice of pulling into pre-stall buffet and avoid the line; or to ease the turn, cross the line, but have a greater safety margin above the stall. In spite of actually infringing the rules, the second method is obviously safer; the final decision is the pilot's alone, and he alone must carry full responsibility.

Low level flying in extreme attitudes brings its own problems. A pilot may be perfectly capable at 1,000 feet of performing a manoeuvre with no height loss. However, he may be concerned with the thought of performing the same manoeuvre at 100 feet, and if he finds himself in a position where, although speed, attitude, power available, and position in front of the crowd are all ideal for the manoeuvre in question, but, because of the low altitude, there is a split second's doubt about his ability to fly it, he must not attempt it! Confidence is a prerequisite of success in low level aerobatics, and if any doubt exists, confidence will be lost, and the manoeuvre will deteriorate; and at really low level this hazard cannot be accepted. It is better to throw it away, and to stay around to fly another day.

In low level flying there is a constant requirement to have available precise height information, and this cannot always be provided by the altimeter, which not only suffers from lag, but because of extreme sideslip and pitch angles, both positive and negative, there are considerable position errors, which cannot easily be measured. We know that many aerobatic aeroplanes have an error when inverted of 200 feet "the wrong way", that is, you are 200 feet nearer the ground than is recorded on the altimeter. Also the airspeed indicator can overread by as much as 20 knots; which is partly why the higher speed (indicated) is needed for outside maneouvres. I personally set minus 100 feet before I start, which helps a little, but it is most important in light aircraft to have a very good idea visually as to how much height is needed for a downward looping manoeuvre. My absolute minimum height in a Stampe for a downward loop is 900 feet, and this means that I do not come below 100 metres. The minimum height in the Pitts is the same, but in spite of its higher wing loading, and higher speed, the symmetrical wing equalises things. It is a very good idea, if the cloudbase is low, not to include any figure which passes through the vertical dive, i.e. complete loops, etc.

One should have at one's disposal a bad weather routine, or "flat" show, which is made up mostly of rolling manoeuvres. The alternative, which I favour, is to know the exact entry speeds and heights used by all the figures, so that I can select my sequence as I go along, two or three manoeuvres in advance. Before I begin any figure, I know exactly what it involves; if there is any doubt, I choose a simple one, but I never attempt an uncertain figure at low altitude. If you are in doubt about the visibility and cloudbase, either just fly past in level flight or stay on the ground.

It is sometimes very hard to withdraw on account of weather if one sees other pilots flying their acts, but it is the mark of the professional that he knows his own limitations and will under no circumstances exceed them. It will certainly earn him the respect of other professional pilots.

Low level aerobatics are different from normal aerobatics in only one respect: the ground! If we make a mistake at altitude, we will lose a mark or so at a competition; the same mistake at a display could also be the last. It can be terrifying to watch an inexperienced display pilot looping off the ground at low speed and having to pull hard on the recovery, sometimes in buffet, to avoid hitting the ground. A lot can be learned by watching the more experienced pilot doing the same manoeuvre; the entry at least 20 knots faster than necessary, a wide easy loop, giving

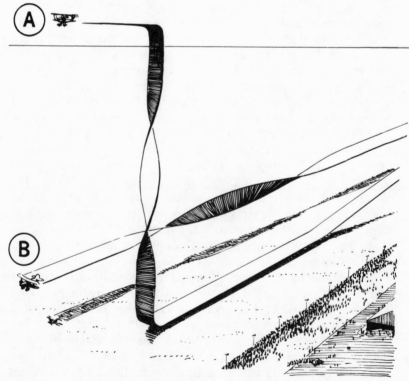

'A' is more spectacular and safer than 'B'

him time to assess whether height is sufficient to continue. In the last half of the loop it becomes obvious that he could pull out at 150 feet if he wanted to, but now he has speed and height in hand he can fly the aircraft right down to the ground in perfect safety. Not only does it look the same from the layman's point of view but he has excess speed ready for the next manoeuvre.

Selection of the right figure is also very important, for example, a vertical roll starting at ground level and flying away at the top in level flight will be more spectacular than a slow roll at 150 feet—and safer!

In general it is a good idea to avoid vertical diving manoeuvres, to use some fairly simple horizontal figures, but mainly concentrate on climbing figures from very low altitude, and then "flying" the aircraft back down under control. These "flydown" manoeuvres are a good area to insert 45° diving half rolls, where the roll rate can be adjusted to make it look very spectacular, but where other professional pilots watching the show will be able to see that the whole situation is well under control.

High quality display flying is by no means as easy as it looks: the fact that it does look easy is a tribute to the skill and discipline of most display pilots. In low level flying there are three kinds of manoeuvres; the easy, the difficult, and the impossible. The aim of the display pilot is to make the easy look spectacular, the difficult look easy, and never to attempt the impossible! There are old pilots, and bold pilots, but no old, bold pilots!

28   *American manoeuvres and terms*

So many people have asked me to explain various American terms that it is perhaps worthwhile having a look at some of these. The two most frequently misunderstood manoeuvres on this side of the Atlantic are probably those simple co-ordination figures, the chandelle and lazy-8. The chandelle properly belongs in the pre-aerobatic training syllabus, although it could with some effect be practiced by a wide range of pilots, because nobody can really say that he doesn't need to fly co-ordination exercises. These figures are of immense value in display flying, as they allow the energy content of the aeroplane to be re-charged whilst still retaining a degree of action in the show.

The chandelle may be described briefly as a climbing turn through 180°. But as one might expect, there is more to it than that! To begin with, it is not necessary to use full power, but the power, once selected, must not be adjusted. It is best flown into wind, since it is easier to associate with a ground feature if this done. From a given speed, the bank is steadily applied, and at the same time a steady climb is initiated, so that when the bank angle has reached 30°, the nose has achieved an attitude of 15° above the horizon, and the aircraft has turned through 30° from the original heading. The bank continues to increase at the same steady rate, as does the pitch, and when the aircraft has turned through 90°, the bank angle is at a maximum of about 60°. Thereafter the bank decreases again at the same steady rate, reaching the wings level position with 180° turned. All this time the nose has been pitching up steadily so that when the wings are once again level, the nose is at its highest point, and the aircraft is flying at the minimum possible speed. During the whole of the manoeuvre the slip ball will have been exactly centred, and the end result is that the aircraft has carried out an exact 180° climbing turn, with the maximum possible height gain. The rate at which the manoeuvre is flown is entirely up to the pilot, but the pitch and bank rates must correspond exactly with each other. Obviously the slower the figure is flown, the more elegant it will appear from the ground.

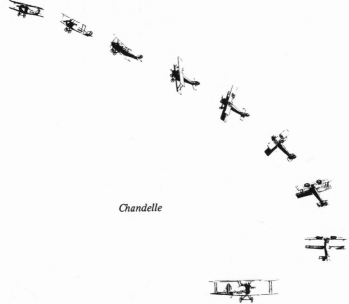

Chandelle

The lazy-8 is not an eight at all, but from above traces the shape of an "S" over the ground. Like the chandelle, it is a precision co-ordination manoeuvre, and has no particular use in an aerobatic display, although it can be flown, even by a non-aerobatic machine for display purposes, and this will allow the quality of the display to be enhanced.

Lazy Eight

This manoeuvre, too, is best flown into wind to preserve the shape, although it can look effective when flown crosswind. It starts as a co-ordinated climbing turn, reaching 45° bank, 45° pitch and 45° turned simultaneously. The climbing turn is continued, reaching about 60° nose up at the 90° point, and with 90° bank achieved. The bank then comes off at the same rate as it went on and the nose starts down again, so that with 45° left to turn to complete the first 180° turn, the nose is 45° down, and the bank is reducing through 45°. As the aircraft reaches the 180° mark, the wings are level and the nose is on the horizon, with the same speed and height indications as were used to start the manoeuvre. This completes half the figure, which, when repeated in the opposite sense, gives the full manoeuvre. As in the chandelle, the slip ball must be central throughout, and the essence of both these figures is smooth accurate flying. Any airspeed in excess of normal cruising speed is suitable to commence these manoeuvres.

Another popular figure in the States, which appears early in their syllabus is called the Split-S. In fact this is a natural continuation of the roll off the top, since it involves simply rolling to the inverted position and pulling through in the second half of a loop. It is also quite common to half flick to the inverted before pulling through. In this country it appears later in the syllabus because it is obvious that if one enters the manoeuvre at too high an airspeed one is going to be faced with a high speed high g situation at the bottom, and we feel that it is a good idea for the student to have become used to this sort of loading over a more prolonged training period.

Some of these manoeuvres are only confusing because they have different titles: they are not really different at all. So it is that a "hammerhead" becomes a stall turn; a "whip stall" is a tail slide, and a "snap roll" is a flick roll.

29 *Aeroplanes for aerobatics*

From time to time a survey of clubs and schools which can teach aerobatics appears in print, and it is reasonable to suppose that any one of these organisations can impart the necessary knowledge. Up to a point, as far as the level of instruction is concerned, this is so. Many of them can supply instructors (possibly ex-military with a CFS background) who can undoubtedly cover the basic figures. However good these instructors are, the level of their potential success depends upon the standard of material available to them. This means that pilots who have had the accent on pure handling in their training will have an advantage over people who have been taught that procedures are paramount. This is great for potential airline pilots, but it seems a pity that so many people who just want to learn to fly, without their realising it at the time, are being groomed for a four-ringed uniform.

There is, additionally another burden on the shoulders of the aerobatic instructor, and that is the aeroplane available to him. Without naming names, most of the aerobatic aeroplanes in this country are low powered tricycle machines, converted or beefed up from normal club trainers. One might argue that apart from the length of time needed to climb to a safe instructional height, there is nothing basically wrong with this. In fact there is one factor which should be borne in mind at all times. These aeroplanes are, in general, only semi-aerobatic, with limit loads of around $+4 \cdot 5g$. The negative limits may be less than $-2g$. This, then, poses some interesting problems for the instructor.

To return for a moment to an aeroplane like the Tiger Moth; given enough height the instructor could let the student make a real hash of it before assuming control, because the drag was so high that the speed was unlikely to get completely out of hand, and the limit load was so high that the student would black himself out long before he could pull enough to damage the aeroplane.

In the case of the semi-aerobatic aeroplane, the instructor dare not let the student go too far, because with its restricted *g* envelope, there is a limit to how hard one may pull, and that limit is not very high. Also these machines are cleaner and will accelerate very rapidly in a steep dive, so that there is even less time to sort it out, because, as we have seen, the *g* limits are further reduced as the speed approaches VNE.

As if that were not enough, the instructor must satisfy himself that the student is competent to stay inside these fairly tight limits before being sent off for solo aerobatics. As a result of all this, the poor student may well be worked up to a fine pitch which will do his aerobatics no real good at all.

The manufacturers in their wisdom have considered the problem of the inadvertent overstress, and to make this slightly harder to achieve they have moved the C.G. forward and reduced the elevator authority, and may even have increased the stick force per *g*. These modifications result in the most ridiculous pressures having to be applied to the control column in order to achieve a reasonable pitch rate, and this is especially noticeable on certain American aerobatic aeroplanes. For the mathematically inclined, it is very interesting to work out the elevator forces required to achieve the maximum permitted *g* at the maximum permitted speed. The forces involved are very high indeed, unless one has, and uses, an elevator trim tab, and there are many reasons why a light aeroplane should not be re-trimmed into the manoeuvre in aerobatics.

When an aeroplane is set up as a stable cruising platform, as semi-aerobatic aeroplanes are, it follows that there will be a big trim change from erect to inverted – yet another problem for the harrassed student! This is alleviated very slightly if the engine continues to give power when inverted, which is not all that common. And remember, we are only discussing basic aerobatics at the moment.

So it seems there is a good case for a fully aerobatic training aeroplane in reasonable numbers which will allow students to make a mistake without breaking the aeroplane or having their confidence shattered by the instructor grabbing the controls at frequent intervals. Such an aeroplane would need at least a limit of $+6$ and $-3g$ with full fuel and two people on board.

There are only three such aeroplanes in production which are available commercially, and they are produced in Czechoslovakia, France, and the USA. They are the Zlin, Cap 10, and Pitts S2A, and of these, only the Zlin and Pitts have been seen in this country. Both of them would make very good trainers, but such has been the pilot indoctrination over the past few years, that only a small percentage of the total number of licenced pilots (and there are about 100,000) are prepared to fly them, for the simple reason that they are tailwheel machines and that they have tandem seating! Now there are some good reasons for adhering to this particular concept when it comes to selecting an aerobatic trainer, as opposed to the usual tricycle side-by-side layout. When we search for a suitable training aeroplane for intermediate work we must always look ahead to the full blooded contest aeroplane, so if we examine those requirements we will understand why the Zlin and Pitts make good trainers.

The best types of aircraft for competitions of world championship standard seem to fulfil certain requirements. The wing loading should be between 8 and 12 pounds per square foot since this will allow a fair distribution between slow controlled flight and flick roll ability. The wing section itself should be symmetrical, or nearly so, thus allowing nearly equal performance inverted as compared with erect flight. At the same time the wing should be fairly thick in the case of a monoplane, which assists slow flight and also gives high drag when required, i.e. in a vertical diving roll. The thick wing also makes life easier for the designer in giving the wing more strength. The biplane is less of a problem, because with its externally braced structure, it can be made immensely strong, and one of the primary requirements of a modern machine will be strength. It should be capable of operating to a limit of $+9$ and $-6g$.

A swept leading edge is desirable to give improved flick roll capability without compromising low speed flight to any extent, and this is often combined with a reduction of dihedral; the effect being to reduce the erect lateral stability, and to improve the inverted lateral stability. The overall result will be a more evenly matched aeroplane regardless of attitude. Engine power is currently between 160 hp and 300 hp, and one aims to achieve a power loading approaching 5 lbs per hp, which is achieved in the Pitts SI-S.

It will be necessary for a biplane to have about 25 per cent more power as compared with a monoplane of the same size and weight to achieve comparable performance, although the biplane will have a pitch capability unmatched by any monoplane, except when interlinked controls are used. Whereas a biplane can get by with conventional controls, if we want a monoplane to be able to fly the same corners, we will have to change the camber of the wing in flight, and this has been achieved on the Akrostar, where the flaps and ailerons droop in the ratio of 2:1 when the stick is pulled back, and vice versa; and the ailerons and flaps operate in a 2:1 ratio when used in the rolling mode. This has caused longitudinal control and stability problems necessitating anti-balance tabs on the flaps, and a wedge on the trailing edge of the all-flying tailplane. It's quite a remarkable aeroplane.

When the size of the machine increases, it is not so important to have linked controls, and when we have a machine the size of the Yak 18 we can get away with it, but we will need 300 hp! A fixed undercarriage is often an advantage, since most of the flying is done at a very low speed. This may sound strange at first, but if we plot speed against time in a sequence we will find that it is so. It follows that the drag of the gear in normal flight can be turned to our advantage when rolling vertically downwards with the throttle closed to conserve height. When fitted with spats, it can provide an extra lifting force in knife flight, slow rolls, etc, and a fixed undercarriage usually results in a much stronger aeroplane in the area of the centre section than if the gear was retractable.

When we talk of power loading, we can achieve our requirement in two ways; increase power or reduce weight. Now because increased power brings the attendant problems of gyroscopic effects, torque and slipstream, we will need more powerful controls to offset these at the same speed, so the obvious way to achieve the same overall result is to reduce weight. This is another reason why we select the tailwheel undercarriage; it is lighter. Finally if we have a fixed tricycle undercarriage the result in inverted flight will be to produce turbulence and disrupted airflow across what is now our primary lifting surface.

By dispensing with a retractable undercarriage we also dispense with the mechanism associated with it, and so we do not need to fit an hydraulic or electrical system. If we are prepared to hand-swing the propeller, we can do without electrical starter, battery, and therefore generator, with a tremendous saving in weight. If handswinging is likely to be a problem, we can accept the weight of a starter plus a plug in point for a ground power unit.

By keeping the C.G. as far back as possible we can effectively increase our pitch and yaw capability, and as a result we will have a less tractable, but more lively aeroplane. However, an aft C.G. can be an embarrassment when it comes to stopping a spin or flick on heading, so we must not go too far in this direction.

A variable pitch propeller means that full power can be used all the time without fear of over-revving the engine, and this will allow the maximum performance to be extracted from the aeroplane.

An extremely important factor is seating position: apart from the obvious fact that the nearer one gets to the reclining position the better one's *g* tolerance, this also means that in inverted flight one is supported by lying on the straps, and under, say, minus 6*g* in an Akrostar, which is so equipped, it is extremely uncomfortable. Also, one's head needs to be orientated normally with respect to the aeroplane, so that in the correct seating position one can turn the head under *g* without effort. It is essential to be seated centrally in the fuselage, as one needs all the visual cues one can get, and in the side-by-side cockpit, there is a large area to the right of the nose which the pilot cannot see. This becomes even more vital in outside manoeuvres, where peripheral vision becomes extremely important. The cockpit should be so located that the pilot can look out laterally along the straight trailing edge of the wing, and in vertical rolls he can track the wing along the line of the horizon in the manner of sighting a gun. You will see aeroplanes with marks and even bits of ironmongery attached to the wingtips as a "sight", but none of them are as good as having the aircraft geometry correct in the first place.

Many so-called fully aerobatic aeroplanes boast two seats, long range, a baggage compartment, and so on. There is enough compromise in the best of aerobatic aeroplanes without adding to it! A really good aerobatic aeroplane can have no other purpose. The Yak 18 has such a small fuel tank that its endurance is about 25 minutes: but that is long enough to fly two or three sequences! It also has the advantage that with a small fuel tank it can be filled before each competition flight, whereas aircraft with larger tanks sometimes have to reduce weight in high temperatures by reducing fuel, and this increases the danger of air bubbles in the fuel lines.

Powerful ailerons giving a high roll rate need no explanation when it comes to vertical rolls, but what is not always so evident

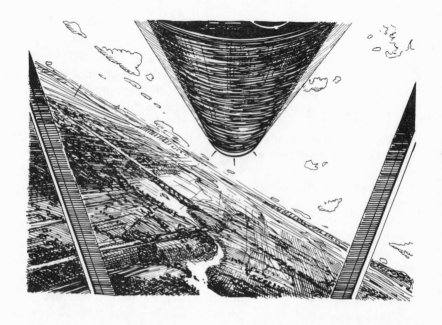

Same ground features as seen from differing types in identical attitudes

is that they are equally necessary in vertical downward rolls, thus allowing the necessary rotation to be made in the minimum height band, and without gaining too much airspeed. In modern flying, we have to draw a line after the roll, and then pull or push into level flight; and it is this pull or push which can break an aeroplane. With our high roll rate we can fly the roll, draw the line, and still not have an excessive speed to make the corner. The Yak, however, with its very clean lines would still be in trouble in spite of its high rate of roll, were it not for the fact that it is equipped with a very powerful airbrake, operated instantly via the aircraft pneumatic system using a button on top of the stick!

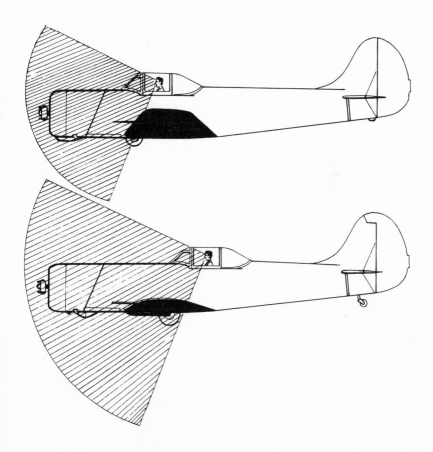

Pilot's cone of vision from different cockpit locations

Because the wing structure is so light on a biplane, in spite of its increased volume, the rolling inertia can be extremely low (one wing of a Jungmeister weighs only 25 lbs). This results in the ability to accelerate very rapidly in the flick roll, and also allows it to stop equally quickly. The very powerful external bracing assembly also permits a high airspeed in flick entry, which gives a much faster and cleaner manoeuvre. With an entry speed of up to 190 km/hr it is small wonder that the Jungmeister is the best flicking aeroplane of all, especially so in the recovery.

Visual density plays a very important part in the makeup of an aerobatic aeroplane, and it is here that the larger machines score. At a height of 1,000 metres, a Yak 18 is clearly visible, while the diminutive Pitts is just a dot in the sky. The larger aircraft appear to fly more slowly than they really do, and this gives them an added quality of grace and ease of flight.

They can use the upper part of the box with impunity, and still be scored high, whereas the tiny Pitts is forced into the lower levels where it can be more clearly seen. As well as visual density it is important to have clean lines, which will make the judges' task easier, since every movement of the aircraft will be clearly defined. This, while being a disadvantage to an inaccurate pilot, will accentuate the skill of the pilot who gets it right. The Zlin, when flown with confidence and precision, is bound to pull in the marks. It becomes obvious that a fixed undercarriage has an extremely important effect on visual appearance, as there can be no doubt as to the attitude of the machine. Even colour is important, and it is common practice to paint the underside of the aircraft all one colour, while the top surface is broken up by sunbursts of two different colours. The British aircraft are red underneath and white on top with blue flashes. This distinctive colour scheme makes it easier for the judges to see the attitude of the aircraft.

It is difficult to separate high noise and high performance; the two usually go hand in hand. Mostly it is not so much the noise of the engine that is a problem but the fact that the propeller tips may be supersonic. A constant speed propeller may be an answer, but it may not be possible to fit such a device to really small aeroplanes without seriously compromising the C.G. In a competition the noise can help because it helps to hold the judges' attention when the aircraft is very high.

We have seen some reasons why the pilot should be situated well back; perhaps the most important reason of all is that he should have as much of the aeroplane visually ahead of him as is possible. Especially on a cloudless day, in an outside manoeuvre, he needs all the visual cues he can get, and as he must keep his head to the front so as not to drop a wing, he must rely on peripheral vision and the mental projection of the intended track of the aeroplane to help him. As he aimed the wingtips around the horizon in a vertical roll, so he must aim the nose in a true arc in an outside loop, and the longer the nose he can see in front of him, the straighter will be the manoeuvre. This is where the Pitts is difficult compared with the Yak or Zlin.

Many aircraft have clear vision panels cut in the floor, and these are mainly intended for tracking along the axes, perhaps when decelerating for a spin. However they can also be used in an outside loop to pick up the axis very early and thus keep straight. They are also very useful before starting the sequence when one uses them as a form of drift sight to assess the wind.

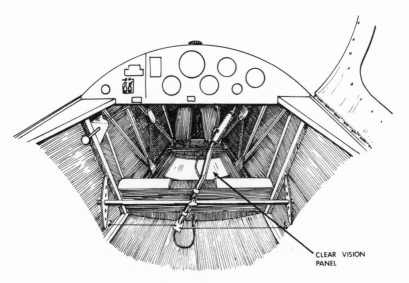

CLEAR VISION PANEL

These days one accepts without question the fact that the engine will continue to run steadily in inverted flight with full oil pressure, but this has not always been so. Many of our present inverted systems originated with the experiments of aerobatic enthusiasts in the early days, and it is interesting to compare the Lycoming aerobatic conversion modifications with our early attempts to

Standard Lycoming Sump

In standard Lycoming aircraft engines oil circulation is entirely internal. Oil from the sump enters the sump screen at the front, passes through the perforations in the sump screen wall, and flows up through the passage at the rear of the sump to the engine oil pump and out to engine lubrication points.

When an aircraft using this type engine is inverted, the oil in the sump falls to the top of the crankcase, and oil pressure is lost immediately since there is no longer a supply to the engine oil pump. In addition, substantial oil loss occurs due to direct flow overboard through the breather line at the top of the engine crankcase (not shown).

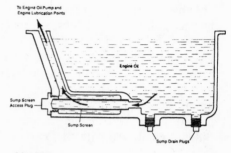

Converted Lycoming Sump

Modification of the Lycoming engine sump to use the Inverted Oil System is accomplished without engine removal or extensive disassembly by simply changing several engine sump parts. The forward end of the sump screen is plugged with the Sump Plug, and the sump screen access plug is replaced with the Sump Fitting. The sump drain plugs are replaced with standard AN and MS fittings which are attached through hoses to other parts of the Inverted Oil System as described on following pages.

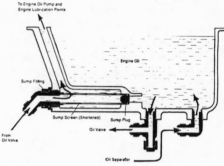

Normal Flight Operation

During normal flight, the weighted ball valve at the top of the Oil Separator is open, allowing blowby gases from the engine crankcase to be vented from the breather port, through the Breather Tee, to the Oil Separator, and out through the overboard breather line. The top port of the Valve is closed, and the bottom port is open, allowing oil to flow from the sump out through the Valve, to the Sump Fitting, and through the sump screen, up to the oil pump and out to engine lubrication points.

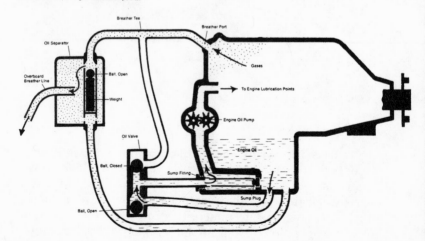

9-13

Inverted Flight Operation

When the aircraft is inverted, engine oil falls to the top of the crankcase. The weighted ball valve in the Oil Separator closes, permitting the engine oil pump to draw oil through the oil valve from the crankcase and preventing overboard loss of oil through the Oil Separator. Blowby gases from the engine crankcase are vented from the sump to the Oil Separator and out through the overboard breather line. The top port of the Oil Valve is open, and the bottom port is closed, allowing oil to flow out from the breather port, through the Breather Tee, to the Oil Valve, through the Sump Fitting and the sump screen, to the oil pump and out to engine lubrication points.

Any oil in lines which fails to return to the sump during the transition between normal and inverted flight drains into the Oil Separator. This oil then returns to the sump from the bottom of the Oil Separator during periods of normal flight.

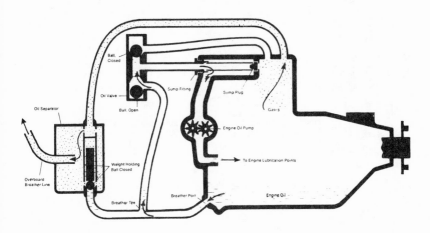

provide the Cosmic Wind with a fully inverted system! This latter utilised a continuous feed system to the carburettor, but it suffered from flooding in certain attitudes with the attendant rich cut. The only way to prevent this from occurring was to turn off the main fuel cock before the cut occurred, and this reduced pump output sufficiently to keep the engine running! It required not only a fine sense of anticipation but also the dexterity of a one-armed paper hanger, as may be imagined from the fact that in addition to all the normal problems, I also had to turn the fuel cock off and on no less than sixteen times during my free sequence in the World Aerobatic Championships in Bilbao, 1964!

How much more simple and efficient is the modern Lycoming system! In nearly all these systems, since gravity is the source of fuel and oil problems when the aeroplane is inverted, it is this same force that we use to correct the situation by means of gravity operated valves and flop tubes.

Since the wellbeing of the engine is of paramount importance to the aerobatic pilot, it follows that a large proportion of the instrument panel will be devoted to the presentation of this

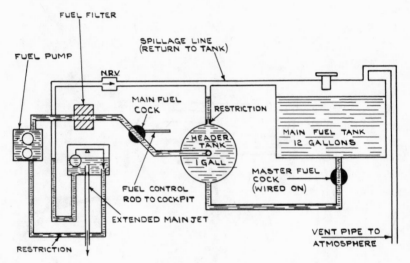

FUEL SYSTEM

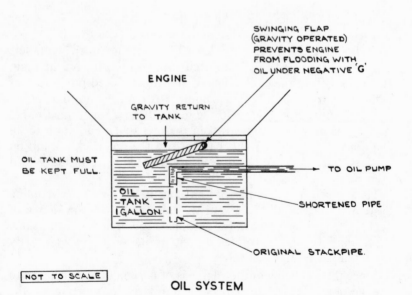

NOT TO SCALE

OIL SYSTEM

Cosmic Wind Fuel and Oil System

information. These instruments can tell a tale as clearly as the printed word to the pilot who is accustomed to reading them. It therefore follows that the best instrumentation layout is not achieved by accident, but rather must be carefully planned, so that when vision is reduced by *g*, the important instruments can still be read. We know that it is not a good thing to turn the head during manoeuvres involving *g* because of the coriolis effects and ensuing disorientation, so we must place the primary references central, where possible. Pride of place must go to the sequence card, which should be large for easy reference. This means that there will be a large area in the centre of the panel where we cannot place essential instruments, so this is the place to install the compass or any navigation equipment or radios, which ought to be de-mountable.

The East Germans have a very neat detachable compass installation for transit flying in their Zlins, and while there may be small errors due to the installation, these are perhaps smaller than those resulting from the forces and rotations in aerobatics.

Above and below the card should be fitted the inverted and erect slip balls: remembering that the head of the pilot is tilted back a little in inverted flight, so we do not wish to make him move his head to see the inverted slip ball. There is also a good case for installing this indicator in the centre section of the top wing, which is just about where the pilot is looking. The accelerometer and stopwatch should also be mounted high up on the panel, and as near to the ASI as possible, as these are the three main parameters we will need to monitor. The altimeter is not so important, as for a large part of the time we cannot rely on it due to lag. Engine pressure and temperature instruments should be placed where they can be easily seen, and should be colour coded to show normal and caution ranges; not just with thin lines, but with bold colours. We may only have a second to check them, and the information must be really clear. Recessed instrument panels are bad because if we are pulling hard with reduced vision, into sun, we may not be able to even see such a panel, much less read the instruments.

Many pilots tend to favour all sorts of additions to provide them with attitude and airspeed information, such as sight lines on the canopy, sight frames on the wingtips, and even string taped to the top wing surface outboard, to indicate the beginning of a tailslide. The problem with such devices is that it concentrates the attention in one area to a very large extent, and since spare attention is usually at a premium in aerobatics, this means that attention which is required elsewhere is not available. Simplification is the real answer, together with a feel for the aeroplane which cannot be fully developed with these devices.

We were told in 1964 that the Russians used their "roller blind" gyro horizons for vertical rolls; indeed when one of their pilots sat in the Cosmic Wind he spent some time looking for a similar instrument and would not believe that we used external references. It is noticeable that the Yak 18PS is not equipped with such an instrument; it would appear that they have reached the same conclusions as ourselves!

When it comes to considering a new design, it is necessary to look at current equipment and to study the good and bad points built into them. We should also realise that in many cases the aeroplane is a development of an old design and not specifically planned from the drawing board for world class aerobatics.

In many cases we find that the stability in yaw and pitch is much too high, as on the Cap 20; which means that excessive speeds must be used to make the aeroplane flick well, with the attendant stressing problems. Also the high longitudinal dihedral causes a large trim shift between normal and erect flight, which results in difficulty in flying rolling circles. The machine looks pretty in flight, but its rounded wing shape does not provide a clear sighting line in vertical rolls. Finally it is so clean that it accelerates rapidly in the vertical diving roll, with the attendant high *g* situation at the bottom. This aeroplane was originally derived from the Emeraude concept.

With the Akrostar, on the other hand it is difficult to comment upon the degree of stability, because how can one measure something which does not exist? The control system (or "steering" system, as it is called) is a masterpiece of engineering in that the stabiliser, flaps, and ailerons are all controlled by the same lever, yet there is no "stiction" in the system. There is no inherent "feel" to the aircraft, and it must be flown entirely visually: if the visibility deteriorates, so does the quality of the Akrostar's performance. With a slight tendency to tipstall in rolling circles, it is still not fully developed. The Akrostar is directly descended from the Danish KZ8.

Czechoslovakia have been building Zlins for many years and their latest venture in the competition field is the Zlin 526 AFS. This differs from its predecessors mainly in the fact that the wings have been clipped by over six feet! This was done primarily to reduce the wing bending moment under *g* which in the extreme situations reached in contest flying had placed an excessive load on the centre sections of the full span machines. An additional mini-aileron was fitted inboard to increase the diving roll performance. The result of the shortened span was to increase the induced drag out of all proportion, and resulted in a large speed loss when high *g* was pulled, and also it could not be flown cleanly away from a stalled condition. From the ground it lacked the grace of the earlier models. One hears on the grapevine that there is a new Zlin on the drawing board called the Zlin 50, and that this will be similar to the old, but very successful Zlin 226. Way back in the dim and distant past the Zlin can be traced through the Bücker Bestmann to the Jungmeister – a noble lineage!

A beautiful and graceful aeroplane to watch in flight is the Yak 18PS. Quiet and powerful, it purrs through the sequences, seemingly without effort, and it is not until one flies the Yak and notes its very high directional stability which in conjunction with its standard wing, makes the positive flick roll a little awkward, that one can appreciate the very high skill and training of the Yak pilots. On the other hand, the standard wing stalls sharply in inverted flight and gives the Yak a startling outside flick roll performance for such a big aeroplane. It too, is not very good in the rolling circle, as it will not fly properly on its side, and it relies on a large energy content for its performance: if it loses speed at low altitude, it takes a long time to build it up again. It is derived from a line of Yak trainers going back to the second war.

For sheer brute force one has to award credit to the Pitts SI-S, the symmetrical winged, four aileron, 180 hp, single-seater. The aeroplane is rather overpowered and is very sensitive directionally, this resulting in a source of error in vertical rolls. Because of its small size it is hard to assess the accuracy of a manoeuvre when seen from the ground, and it lacks the grace of the larger machines. It does not have any problems except that of over-controlling by the pilot. The Pitts is a post-war sporting design which has been re-engined many times.

A machine which was seen only briefly in this country was the Spinks Akromaster. This was a single seat low winged monoplane of all metal construction powered by a 200 hp Lycoming engine. It was probably the nearest thing to an updated Zlin 226 that we have seen and was a delight to fly. Outside performance was very impressive with the symmetrical wing and the only disadvantages were the mediocre negative flick roll, due to the aircraft's reluctance to stall inverted, and the positive *g* tipstall in the rolling circle, due to the absence of washout. It was an only prototype, and it is a pity that it was not continued.

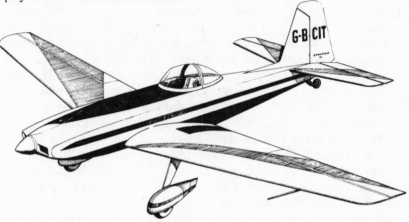

The Cranfield A.1.

Armed with the information and deficient areas of current aerobatic aeroplanes, we were able to lay down a design specification for a competitive British aeroplane. It was decided that the machine would be a single seater with a tailwheel type fixed undercarriage. The prototype will be powered by a Continental 210 hp engine driving a Hartzell VP propeller. No flaps are to be fitted to preserve strength and keep the weight down, and controls will be conventional. The aircraft will be quite large to provide good visual density and will be cleared to limit loads of $+9$ and $-6g$.

Wind tunnel tests were carried out and showed great promise, so work was started at Cranfield, at the Institute of Technology. It is now progressing well, and all weight estimates are being adhered to or bettered.

As work goes on, the detailed design is keeping comfortably ahead, and such was the original concept that it has not been found necessary to alter the initial design, which continues to meet all modern competition requirements. It is turning out to be a very handsome aeroplane, and it is the only fully aerobatic aircraft ever to be designed and built in this country.

It has been said many times about aeroplanes that "if it looks right, it flies right". The Cranfield A1 project certainly does look right, and she will soon be able to prove herself in the air.

30 *At the competition*

During the months of training for the competition, we have scarcely been looking further ahead than the end of the day's flying as we work with tape recorder and tracking board, practicing, studying, learning, and trying again. The compulsory sequence will have been flown many times until the figures are almost automatic, and the free programme will have seen many alterations and improvements. But for the last few weeks the design has been frozen, as we concentrate on trying to fly it perfectly.

Suddenly, with a quickening of the pulse, we realise there is to be no more training, the competition date is only a few days away: now its the real thing! Inevitably we feel anything but ready, and there is a great temptation to train furiously in these last few days, as though it will make any difference! The answer is, it won't – so relax! It is much better to take a couple of days off just before the contest, because the phrase "over-trained" does not always imply a great level of skill and ability. One will usually do better as the result of a rest.

Apart from all the arrangements to be made as far as the route is concerned to the contest site we have to make sure that we are prepared with all our competition documentation, pilot's licence, aircraft papers, insurance, competition licence, entry forms, etc. Don't forget to pack the Aresti dictionary, it can be very useful! The free sequence by now should be clearly tabulated, because when we get there we may have to draw out several detailed copies, and that would be no time to discover a mathematical error!

With the aircraft polished until it is gleaming, for we are our country's representatives here at the contest, we fly a steady, careful circuit on arrival. This is not the place to indulge in careless or extrovert behaviour, for we are inevitably under scrutiny. The discipline required of any aerobatic pilot who deserves the name, is of the highest standard.

As we taxi in, we will see rows of brightly painted aeroplanes of many different nationalities, flown by pilots of international repute, but who are, above all, sportsmen in the best sense of the word. Any of these pilots would be only too ready to help another, even if it meant that by loaning tools, spares, or assistance he might reduce his own chances.

With the greetings and documentation over, we are allocated accommodation and we can relax and renew old acquaintance-ships. This is also a good time to vist the meteorological office and study the forecast for the next few days, with particular attention to the wind velocity.

There will be innumerable briefings, which inevitably start late, but it is nevertheless only good manners to be there on time. Here we draw for training schedules, and we will usually be permitted one flight in the local area and one over the contest area. During the first of these we can run through our sequences primarily to "blow the dust off" after several days' straight and level flying, but mainly to reduce the amount of adrenalin which has been steadily building up in our nervous system! Perhaps the most important aspect of these flights is to have a look at the layout of the "box" with respect to the area immediately around the airfield, and to make a mental note of any prominent landmarks. Later, we will compare this information with a close study of a large scale map of the airfield.

During the training flight over the field we may wish to fly one's sequence, but the most important thing is to get used to the appearance of the "box" from high, medium and low altitude, both erect and inverted, and to fly up and down the two axes, using basic manoeuvres in any sequence that comes to hand to ensure that one is perfectly orientated with respect to the local area.

When you land, every detail that you have seen should be imprinted on your mind, and you should go over it mentally, again and again. Make a note where the sun is going to be in relation to the axes both in the morning and late afternoon; at some points in the sequence it may be the only reference feature you have. Several pilots, before landing, pull off a really spectacular manoeuvre to intimidate the opposition. It can be an effective psychological gambit, but you had better make very sure that you don't fluff it!

With the contest proper under way, one can still learn by watching the other pilots; if one manoeuvre seems to be giving trouble in the known sequences, it may be that there is an element of disorientation due to insufficient ground features to use as reference points, and we may be able to think of another approach to avoid this problem. We can see how other competitors fare in the prevailing wind and we can plan our own wind adjustments accordingly. Try not to let the nervous tension build up: remember that every pilot must be under the same pressures: all except the current World Champion, and for him the pressure is almost intolerable.

It is difficult to relax sufficiently to fly as we did in training, and here experience can help, but it is really all in the mind. We will find that we do not even feel high g, and we will stare unbelievingly at the accelerometer after landing. Try not to hurry the sequence, and don't aim to fly differently to the training flights; otherwise why train? If possible, use the sequence card, even if you know the sequence backwards; in the heat of the contest that may be just the way you would otherwise fly it!

The unknown sequence brings its own problems. Here each team chooses a manoeuvre and the judges put them together in a theoretically flyable sequence; but sometimes the judges have to choose a linking manoeuvre, and these have been known to be more difficult than the actual original figures themselves! Now is the time when those pilots who really know their aeroplanes have a chance of increasing their score. Since we are not allowed to train for this sequence we must draw on our past experience to remember how to fly the figures or to work out how they should be done. Also we must decide on the starting height with the knowledge of the height loss of each manoeuvre. As if that were not enough, we must make what may be an "unflyable" sequence look smooth and controlled, and we must keep it in the "box". A "late" draw helps here, if we could but arrange it, so that we have time to see how other pilots approach the problem. In many cases these manoeuvres will have been selected, not because a team knows how to fly them, but in the almost certain knowledge that other aircraft will have trouble with them! This can, however, backfire in a big way, because one national team selected a stick forward tail slide to give trouble to the opposition, and then suffered the embarrassment of seeing two of its own pilots score zero through falling the wrong way! Just recently a foreign pilot complained to me about the difficulty of flying a particular rolling circle. I was almost sympathetic until I realised that his team had selected the manoeuvre!

There is a great opportunity to cause despondency amongst other teams by what is known as "gamesmanship". Everybody tries, this and it is really only the very experienced who are impervious to it! Such an opportunity came our way at a French International competition, when there was a dispute about the unknown compulsory sequence. It was suggested that it was difficult, or dangerous, or both, and the matter was put to the vote.

Since the French team voted that the sequence should be changed, we considered that regardless of our vote, the alteration would in fact be made, the other nations being roughly equally divided in their vote. As none of us at that time spoke any French, I briefed the team manager that we would be quite happy to fly the original sequence as drawn on the blackboard in the briefing room. He stood up and said his piece, and then sat down amidst a stunned and pregnant silence. This reaction seeming to me to be a bit severe, I asked him what he had said. It turned out that he had simply remarked "you draw it, we'll fly it"!

This absolutely shattered the other teams from a psychological point of view; and that year we did rather well!

Tactics, then, play a large part in modern competitions, but at the same time, one can merely get on with the job of flying and ignore everything else: it is all a question of taste.

All of this, however, can be seen by the casual observer who attends the briefings and mixes with the pilots: it still doesn't answer the question "What is it like to fly in a World Championship?"

So let us take a look at a typical sequence at a World Championship as seen through the eyes of a Zlin pilot, as he waits his turn to fly.

There is a growing impatience, a feeling of "let's get on with it". With so many pilots, it is inevitable that each group will take two days to fly off, and this exercises all the patience that the contestants can muster. As one's turn approaches one is conscious of the speed of events being too rapid. Pilots pace up and down on the tarmac, oblivious of their audience, "flying" their sequence with their hands, estimating wind strength, drift, aircraft attitude to maintain the correct flight path, and the "feel" of the sequence, with regard to timing, flow and ryhthm. Even the old hands, one is glad to see, suffer from nerves at this stage.

Only the Russians, drilled to perfection, are calm. They will fly as they did in practice, with precision and accuracy, compensating for wind and adjusting their flight paths to suit the judges. It is all worked out beforehand; the pilot is a part of the machine. The previous competitor is taxying out; it is time to get ready. The aircraft is already preflighted and fully fuelled; we need the full head of fuel to ensure steady running while inverted.

In the cockpit, seat and rudder are carefully adjusted, and the harness is pulled as tight as possible. Loose strap ends are tucked away, and the sequence card and competition numbers are clipped to the instrument panel.

Photographers move towards the aircraft, and one is grateful to see the team manager intercept them — there must be no break in concentration at this stage. The growl of the Yak overhead is distracting, and one tries to ignore it; it is far too late now to worry about whether he is flying well or badly.

The ground crew give a thumbs up; master switch on, mags on, throttle set, and the prop begins to move as the starter clutch whines. With a crackle the Walter engine fires and settles down to a steady throb. One begins to relax; the Yak is now inaudible.

While the engine warms up, a final check is made on cloud movement, with reference to the axes. The aircraft is then taxied out to the runway caravan, where the card showing the competition number is handed to the controller. The Yak is landing; its time to go. One is still aware of tension. A green light shines from the caravan, and the stopwatch is started as the brakes are released.

The climb pattern has been planned, and the height is checked every 30 seconds in the climb to confirm performance. A square circuit is flown and the drift checked on each leg. The nervousness has now given way to excitement, which in turn is suppressed. The controls are released, and then held lightly, as relaxed as possible. Respiration is carefully controlled; there is a danger here of hyperventilation.

The aircraft is now turning on to the axis and the wings are rocked as we roll into the initial dive to signify that we are about to start.

The sequence has been flown many times before, in training, and we rely on this experience now, as we attempt to keep the aircraft on the axis, inside the "box". For each infringement there is a severe points penalty, while going below 50 metres results in disqualification. If a manoeuvre is omitted one is

'T' minus twelve seconds

scored zero for the figure. If the sequence is flown with a direction error of 180°, everything after the error was made is scored zero. One mistake, even a small one, can cost the pilot ten places.

There is no time to think of the handling of the aircraft; this must be automatic. One is not conscious of physical discomfort, such is the level of concentration.

The judges, nine in all, watch with meticulous attention. Each error, each deviation from line, every move the pilot makes is seen and marked accordingly. The two highest and two lowest scoring judges will have their marks discounted, while the remainder are averaged. A judge may not mark his own country's pilots

At last the sequence is finished. Months of hard work, planning, training, hoping, have come to fruition in one ten minute flight. One mistake will cost the pilot dearly.

We turn finals, double-check the undercarriage, because we know from experience how exhausting contest flying can be. Once down we are grateful to be able to open the canopy and get some cool air. We look for the other pilots to check that the performance looked satisfactory from the ground, and climb rather shakily from the cockpit. It will be an hour or so before one's system returns to normal, and the adrenalin is finally dissipated.

Then comes the period of waiting, alternating between hope and despondency until the score is notified. One alternates between watching the other competitors, trying to assess their level of skill, and making furtive visits to the scoreboard, as the suspense becomes almost unbearable. Only a really good performance will keep all the pilots away from that infernal scoreboard.

This, then is the sport of aerobatics, perhaps the ultimate union between science and art, where men can all but bring a machine to life, and a machine in turn can bring to a man some of the highest pinnacles of achievement and self expression which he can experience. There is no limit to what he can learn, and the aeroplane will open the door to an unending vista of beauty and knowledge. Here a man can know peace, loneliness, happiness, fear, triumph, and despair. It is not a sport for the timid, nor is there room here for the conceited. The road to success is not easy, and perhaps this is why it holds such an attraction in man's imagination.

The ocean of air has many of the qualities of the ocean of water which surrounds our island home; it can offer breathtaking spectacle, restful tranquillity, or it can be cruel and vicious, affording no mercy. From time immemorial man's restless spirit reached out to conquer both sea and air, but they guard their secrets jealously, and release them only to those who have the courage and determination to explore. To men of adventure they are like a drug; one cannot go back. Many potential adventurers dabble in the shallows, but only those who go on to explore the deeps shall eventually reach their goal.

To reach the top one must make many sacrifices; there can be no compromise: the stakes are too high. And yet the ultimate goal in aerobatics is within the reach of anyone; if he will but try! Of course it can be risky; but there was never anything worth doing in this world that did not entail some element of risk. Yet it requires that a man has imagination before he can appreciate that a risk exists, and to be a good aerobatic pilot a man must have imagination.

In this sport such a man is faced with stark reality, and in the end it is not just the ability to make an aeroplane respond with grace and precision to his touch which he will discover, but something far more important: the harsh truth about himself!